WORLD PEACE

'Really'
One Mind @ A Time

WORLD PEACE

'Really'
One Mind @ A Time

Ron Medved & Gregg Cochlan
with Beverley Fast

Medved, Ron

    World peace, really! : one mind @ a time / Ron Medved & Gregg Cochlan ; Beverly Fast, editor.

Includes index.
ISBN 978-0-9867008-0-4

    1. Peace--Psychological aspects. 2. Coexistence--Psychological aspects. 3. Cognitive psychology. 4. Pacific Institute (Seattle, Wash.).
I. Cochlan, Gregg, 1957- II. Medved, Ron, 1944- III. Title.

HM1126.M447 2010   303.6'6019   C2010-905414-8

First edition September 2010

Copyright 2010 Ron Medved and Gregg Cochlan

All rights reserved. No part of this book may be reproduced, transmitted in any form or by any means electronic, mechanical, photocopying, recording or otherwise, or stored in an information storage and retrieval system, without prior written permission from the authors.

An application to register this book for cataloguing has been submitted to the Library of Congress.

World Peace, Really!™ is a registered trademark of Ron Medved and Gregg Cochlan

Cover design by Roberto Morales
Interior design and layout by The Noblet Design Group, Regina, Saskatchewan
Photo by Liz Josias
Printed in Canada by Friesens Corporation, Altona, Manitoba

DEDICATION

The journey toward *World Peace, Really!* began for us with an introduction to Lou and Diane Tice, leaders, mentors and dear friends. They founded The Pacific Institute® in 1970 based on their belief that individuals have a virtually unlimited capacity for growth, change and creativity. Through TPI, and through the model Lou and Diane have presented, we have grown to understand the true dimensions of diversity. This book is our chance to take what we have learned and pay it forward by directing it at a cause we strongly believe in. It is also a thank you, a love letter to Lou, Diane and The Pacific Institute for the education and the inspiration that have led to this book.

TABLE OF CONTENTS

Foreword 5

**Thinking Your
Way to Peace** 6
   Peace. It's A Personal Story 6
   Preaching To The Choir 7
   Getting Started 7
   The Intersection Of 3 Concepts 8
   Peace Is An Inside Job 9
   The Seven Principles 10
   Moving From Thinking To Acting 11
   Discovering A New Vantage Point 12

**Principle 1:
Coexistence Is Our Goal** 14
   Yeah, But Is Peace Really Possible? 15
   Change The Belief, Release The Potential 16
   Fight For Peace? 18
   Or Relax Into Peace? 20
   To Change Your Belief, Understand How Your Mind Works 21
   Coexistence And Ego Identity 24
   Labeling: The First Act Of Violence 25
   Reflective Questions 28

**Principle 2:
Blindness is Our Problem** 30
   Your Perception Of Truth 31
   Disarming Your Mind 34
   Your Place In The "Kosmos" 36
   The Scary Possibilities Of Partially Right 38
   Creating Heroes And Villains 39
   Blind Spots Impact World Peace 42
   Scotoma-Busting 45
   Reflective Questions 46

Principle 3:
Diversity is Our Strength **48**
    The World Is Converging ... On Our Doorstep 50
    Is The World Becoming More Or Less Tolerant? 51
    Challenge Your Comfort Zone 52
    Darwin, Diversity & Survival... 54
    Blinding Ourselves To Diversity 56
    Be A Disputer... 56
    Dialogue Not Discussion... 59
    Reflective Questions... 62

Principle 4:
Normal is Our Enemy **64**
    A World Gone MAD 64
    Normal For You 66
    How Did I Get Here? 68
    Where Normal Gets Its Power.. 71
    When Normals Collide 73
    Bing! You Are Now Crossing A Threshold.................... 75
    Creating A New Normal 78
    Reflective Questions... 82

Principle 5:
Love Is Our Journey **84**
    Non-Judgment, Forgiveness And Love........................... 85
    Hate Is Also A Journey 86
    How Fear Gets In The Way Of Love 88
    Why Fear Is A Barrier 90
    The War Starts Inside 93
    Expand The Gap Between Stimulus And Response 96
    Love Begins With Healing 97
    The Goal Comes First.. 98
    Ignore The "How", For Now...100
    Reflective Questions...102

Principle 6:
Adventure Is Our Friend **104**
    Throw Yourself Out Of Order 106
    Alert Your Mind To The Possibility 107
    Affirm The Goal 109
    Bump! Conflict Is Unavoidable......................................109

Bark! Anger Is Manageable 111
Bing! Competition Can Be Good Or Bad 112
Building Your Efficacy 114
Welcome To Global Citizenship, Make Us Better........... 116
Don't Just Do Something, Stand There 117
Reflective Questions.. 118

Principle 7:
Optimism Is Our Choice **120**
Cynics, Idealists And Optimism 122
Optimism Is A Choice Because Optimism Is Learned ... 124
How Do I Choose Optimism? 126
Step #1: Set The Goal 126
Step #2: Manage Your Self-Talk.................................... 128
Step #3: Use Affirmations To Create An Upward Spiral 129
Spiral Dynamics And Your Kosmic Address.................. 132
Making The Paradigm Shift 134
Welcome To The Balcony 136
Reflective Questions.. 137

Really. **138**
Efficacy, Cause And The Peace Matrix......................... 139
The Characteristics Of Success: Positive Deviance 141
A Double-Dog Dare 143
Apply The Seven Principles 146
It's Time To Start Your Journey 146
What Next? 147

Epilogue **149**
The Pacific Institute.. 149
Wanted: 1,000 Peace Projects 149

Endnotes.. **151**

Index **154**

Acknowledgements... **159**

About the Authors.. **160**

FOREWORD

Several years ago, we became fascinated with the concept of coexistence and, more importantly, the growing challenge of living peacefully in a world growing smaller by the day. We felt strongly that we could make a difference, inspired by The Pacific Institute's proven experience in helping bring peace to Northern Ireland, South Africa, Guatemala, South Central Los Angeles and other places. Cognitive psychology could come to the rescue if more people understood the core concepts. We know we can bring a reasonableness, a fresh perspective to conflicts, whether around the world or right in our own backyards. We feel a responsibility to share what we have learned in the cause of promoting world peace, or at least more peaceful coexistence.

Writing a book is a big goal and this book has been several years in the making. That being said, *World Peace, Really!* is not our end-goal. We not only want the book to be read by thousands of people, we intend the book along with our education and process to be a catalyst for 1,000 peace projects, big and small, throughout the world. This brings us to our challenge. We're asking you not only to read the book, but also to pass it along and encourage others to read it. Then we double-dog-dare you to go one step further – be one of the 1,000 projects happening around the world.

Ron Medved   Gregg Cochlan

"Live as if you were to die tomorrow. Learn as if you were to live forever."
Mahatma Gandhi
Spiritual, political and civil rights leader

THINKING YOUR WAY TO PEACE

World Peace, Really! takes you on a journey to where world peace really begins – inside your own mind.

This book builds on our shared knowledge and experience applying some of the most profound concepts in cognitive psychology to the cause of peace. The book is designed to get you thinking about peace in a practical way. But it is not a workbook about the seven steps to peace, nor is it a book about how you should behave. *World Peace, Really!* is about how your mind works and how peace is really possible when you apply your mind to it.

This book asks you to think about your thinking.

PEACE. IT'S A PERSONAL STORY

The book focuses on the "why" behind your attitudes and beliefs. We show you how to decode your own behavior and recognize the mental barriers that can derail the peace process within you and in the world. We reveal the mental traps you can fall into and provide knowledge and skills to get yourself out again. *World Peace, Really!* is about creating a better world from the inside out. It is a journey, one that will take you where peace really begins – inside your own mind.

PREACHING TO THE CHOIR

Who is this book for? Publishers always want to know the answer to that question. Our first instinct was to say, "Everybody!" But the reality is that we are preaching to choir. We are talking to you. *World Peace, Really!* is for people who want peace, who believe peace is possible, who may already be playing a role in making peace happen – whether at a personal level or on a larger stage. We are talking to people like you, people who want to be able to talk about cultural and religious differences without fear of violence, people who want to turn on the news and hear reasoned reporting rather than sensationalism, people who want to coexist peacefully with other ideas in a world that is growing smaller by the minute. This book is for you.

GETTING STARTED

Did you know that "world peace" is one of the most searched phrases on Google? It sounds impossibly of motherhood and apple pie, and yet people really are interested – people in your neighborhood, in the next state or province, even half-way around the world. World peace is a concept that lives in our hearts and minds. But is it really possible? We think so.

World Peace, Really! is based on our experiences working with individuals, organizations and communities as they work to improve performance, build efficacy and reach their potential. The idea of a book on world peace has been percolating inside us for some time, on different, yet parallel tracks. Gregg is a Canadian,

Ron is an American. Gregg is interested in how conflict manifests itself as deviation from the normal and how our perception of normal is actually a catalyst for conflict. Ron is interested in coexistence as a practical response to living together despite social, cultural, religious and political differences. Our work has brought us together in many spontaneous and animated discussions, and when one of these conversations hit on world peace, we discovered a shared desire to really do something about it.

THE INTERSECTION OF 3 CONCEPTS

We propose a path to peace based on the intersection of three concepts – cognitive psychology, the translation and application of cognitive psychology through The Pacific Institute® (TPI) education, and our concept of coexistence as something that begins in your own mind. Our seven principles, which we will introduce in a few moments, show you how this intersection of ideas can help you think your way to peaceful coexistence.

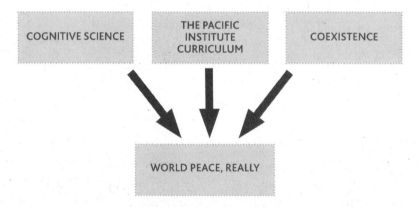

Cognitive psychology explores the impact of the mind on learning and behavior. It gives us insights into how our minds perceive, reason, learn and "know". TPI has a 40-year track record of working with the world's leading cognitive scientists, translating and applying their findings to education and tools that have transformed individuals, organizations and communities. Together, we have close to 50 years experience delivering TPI education around the world. We have seen it generate positive change at every level.

We live what we teach, and that has brought us to this book. Our seven principles present the knowledge and tools you need to advance the cause of peace from the inside out. You will learn how your beliefs and your perceptions of "normal" impact your capacity for peace. You will learn to recognize previously hidden-in-plain-sight "blind spots", how your ingrained habits, attitudes, beliefs and expectations can derail your best intentions, and how to use Gestalt and goal setting to get back on the peace train.

PEACE IS AN INSIDE JOB

Our goal in the following chapters is to help you see world peace as a practical possibility. The principles – call them rules of conduct, natural laws or fundamental truths – are not new in themselves; cultures around the world have promoted them in one form or another for thousands of years. This is something we frequently see in our work. Several years ago, for example, Ron was a guest at a seminar hosted by a long-time client in Saudi Arabia. At one point, a participant stood and said, "You know, this is nothing new. Everything you are saying is in the Koran." Yes! And we have had Christian pastors and Jewish rabbis say exactly the same thing – this is our truth too, they tell us. So if these are truths we all share, why do we get into such terrible conflict with each other?

The biggest "ah-ha" for us in writing this book was that peace – world peace – begins on the inside. You have to believe in peaceful coexistence in your mind, at the thought level. You can help or hurt peace by the way you think. But first, you need to understand how your mind works. We believe this should be part of basic education, something taught from a young age just as reading, writing and arithmetic are taught. So much would be improved if we all knew why we think and act the way we do, and if we all had the knowledge and tools to manage our own minds. It is a lesson everybody needs to learn – everybody in the world.

THE SEVEN PRINCIPLES

Cultural, religious, economic, social and philosophical beliefs may differ widely, but our knowledge of how the human mind works is constant. In the following chapters, we draw on that to show you how to use the seven principles to make peace an active part of your everyday life. The more you find ways to practice peace, the more you will become an instrument of peace.

1. **Coexistence is Our Goal:** Coexistence means existing together in peace, at the same time, in the same place, despite cultural, economic, religious, social or other differences. It is the first and foremost principle of *World Peace, Really!* We'll show you how believing in peace really can make it happen.

2. **Blindness is Our Problem**: Principle 2 is about digging deeper into how the mind works to reveal the tricks and traps that can undermine your ability to peacefully coexist with other ideas, other cultures, other beliefs. It is all about identifying and challenging your blind spots.

3. **Diversity is Our Strength:** This principle is about challenging your comfort zones, discovering the difference between dialogue and discussion, and learning to dispute the information fed to you about "other" ideas, people, cultures. Diversity is not something to be afraid of – diversity is a strength.

4. **Normal is Our Enemy**: If you thought "normal" was a good thing, think again. Your perception of normal plays a powerful role in your ability to peacefully coexist. We'll show you why. We'll also show you what you can do about it.

5. **Love is Our Journey**: After exploring how your mind works, identifying your blind spots, uncovering your barriers to diversity and coming to grips with the power of your normal, this is where we ask you to start applying the principles to building a more peaceful world. Your journey begins with love.

6. **Adventure is Our Friend:** World peace is an awfully big adventure, so big it is tempting to shrink from it. That's a mistake. Too often, you set goals based on what you believe you can achieve right now, with the resources you already have. We believe in setting goals based on what you really want. Make it so vivid you can taste it. Don't worry about how, focus on what. That's the adventure.

7. **Optimism is Our Choice**: You have the tools to look beyond your blindness, to challenge your normals and embrace coexistence. You are filled with love and ready for adventure. You are beginning to create a better world from the inside out. Now, how to sustain your transformation? We'll show you how to make optimism your choice.

MOVING FROM THINKING TO ACTING

Dr. Al Bandura, an eminent Stanford University psychologist, is known for his landmark research on efficacy. Efficacy is the belief that you can cause something to happen, and it plays a major role in moving you from thinking about a thing to acting on it. We introduce him here because we want to share with you the outcome of a remarkable interview between Dr. Bandura and Ron. In this interview, Dr. Bandura outlined four steps he believes are necessary to successfully spread new knowledge. These steps demonstrate the role you can play in helping move the world from thinking about world peace to acting on it.

Theory – The seven principles are based on sound research in cognitive psychology. We are not promoting any one brand of cognitive theory, but many theories, each of which contributes to our understanding of how the mind works.

Translation – A good theory needs to be translated into education before it can be successfully shared. This is what Lou Tice did when he founded The Pacific Institute: he translated the principles of cognitive science into applicable, understandable language so that individuals and organizations could use them.

Implementation – Our first-hand experience has proven the value of the TPI education model, which offers a variety of delivery systems, including implementation strategies for organizations. This book is our way of advancing the cause of peace, our website and workshops are another. But we also want to encourage an even more powerful implementation delivery system … all of us.

Diffusion – Diffusion is simply about spreading the word and sharing the knowledge and tools put forward in our seven principles with others. We start with good theories, translate them into knowledge and implement them through teaching, workshops, projects, print and online media. But it is up to you to practice it; this is when the process of social change really begins to expand into families, neighborhoods, communities, social groups and nations.

DISCOVERING A NEW VANTAGE POINT

Picture yourself standing on a balcony overlooking a dance floor – the dance floor is your life and you can see yourself move across it. There are different level balconies; as you climb higher, each new balcony offers a broader perspective. You see things you had not noticed on the dance floor, or even on lower balconies: how your actions impact the people around you, how you interact with them, how they respond to you, even the ripple effects of your actions. You see it all, but you see it objectively. The hurt, anger and frustration fade away as you climb higher. You see that the human race, for all our differences, is one race. On the outside, we are all different. On the inside, we are all the same. Our lungs breathe air, our hearts pump blood, our minds think new thoughts. It is the kind of epiphany astronauts say they experience when looking back at the earth from space. We are all one people.

Learning how your mind works will help you discover a new, more objective vantage point. It is the kind of self-knowledge you need to reach the balcony and climb to even higher balconies.

World Peace, Really! is our contribution to the peace process. Our hope is that the principles outlined here find their way into your everyday routine. It is a big goal for a slim book, but you can help make it happen by paying forward the principles you learn here. Implement them, share them, live them. Together, we can make peace happen … one mind at a time.

"General, you are going to have to find yourself a new enemy."
Mikhail Gorbachev to Colin Powell
1987 U.S.-U.S.S.R. Summit

PRINCIPLE 1:
COEXISTENCE IS OUR GOAL

Coexistence means existing together in peace, at the same time, in the same place, despite cultural, economic, religious, social or other differences. It is the first and foremost principle of World Peace, Really! In this chapter, we'll show you how believing in peace really can make it happen.

What makes your blood boil – right-wing politics, left-wing politics, cultural profiling, religious fundamentalists, atheists, the debate on climate change, talk of health care reform, corporate bail-outs? We live in interesting times. Overwhelmed by information, we intuitively respond yes or no, I agree or I don't agree to the constant flow of news and opinions being pushed at us. The result is that we, as communities and countries, are becoming increasingly partisan and polarized. Trash talking is everywhere. We loudly cheer our own opinions and just as loudly mock anyone who disagrees. I win, you lose; I'm right, you're wrong. This might be coexistence but it is non-peaceful coexistence, and it is taking a toll on our economies, environment, society and personal lives.

Peaceful coexistence means existing together in peace, at the same time, in the same place, despite any differences we might have. It can apply to two people stuck in an elevator or two billion people living under a common flag. It does not matter who you are or where you live, we believe peaceful coexistence is essential to your health and well-being.

Wishing for world peace and getting involved in making it happen on a day-to-day level are interconnected. We talk about world peace at a macro-level: nations, religions, politics, philosophies and more. But we also challenge you to live world peace at a micro-level – in your interactions with family, friends, coworkers and community.

YEAH, BUT IS PEACE REALLY POSSIBLE?

Gregg: In the late 1990s, I had a chance to hear a keynote address by Colin Powell, who had been the National Security Advisor under U.S. President Ronald Reagan. My world view was still maturing at the time. I had a prejudice toward the military and military might, so I wasn't expecting to be engaged by Powell's talk. Boy, was I wrong. His passion for serving his country broke down my barriers, but it was his story about participating in summit talks with Soviet president Mikhail Gorbachev that really got me. Powell had lived his entire life believing the Soviet Union was the "Enemy", and containment of communism was at the core of his military career. In his talk to us, he vividly recalled a point in the 1987 summit when Gorbachev looked at him across the table and said, "My dear friend and comrade, all I can say is you are going to need to find a new enemy." It meant the end of the Cold War and a chance for peace, but Powell's overwhelming reaction was, "Aw shit, I don't want a new enemy: I'm happy with the one I've got." It was an "ah-ha" moment for me. It made me realize just how strange and powerful our past conditioning can be, because it can actually make it hard for us to believe in world peace.

Colin Powell's story of meeting with Gorbachev is a compelling example of coexistence. The global benefits of ending the Cold War are clear, but more telling from our perspective is the level of discomfort the entire process created at the micro level, within Colin Powell and others with similar conditioning. Instead of joyfully accepting the idea that nuclear war between East and West was not inevitable, decision-makers had to be shocked into a different world view by a man bold enough to propose peace. The "ah-ha" is that world peace is an achievable goal; that is the beginning, the belief that it is possible.

CHANGE THE BELIEF, RELEASE THE POTENTIAL

The first step in your journey toward world peace is establishing in your own mind that peace is possible. Establish the belief and you free your mind to live up to that belief. We have seen it happen time and again. Cognitive psychology tells us that **our minds act in accordance with the truth as we believe and perceive it to be**[1]. Remember this phrase; it is a key learning that opens the door to everything that follows.

Your mind acts in accordance with the "truth" as you believe and perceive it to be. Believing world peace is possible releases the potential for making world peace possible.

How is acting in accordance with the truth as you believe and perceive it to be relevant to coexistence? What you believe affects how you work, live, treat yourself and treat others. Your beliefs not only tell you what kind of person you are, they tell you what kind of people "they" are; what you are capable of doing and what "they" are capable of doing; how kind-honest-trustworthy you are and how kind-honest-trustworthy "they" are. To get to coexistence, you need to take accountability for improving the way you think about yourself and your world. When you expand limiting beliefs or alter negative beliefs, you can release the potential inside you to move toward world peace.

BELIEF & SELF-REGULATION[2]

One of the foundations of cognitive psychology is that your beliefs are formed by the way you think. You think in three dimensions: words that trigger pictures that trigger emotions. Words – pictures – emotions. This form of thought is called self-talk and it is going on inside your mind all the time.

In an average day, you might have 50,000 thoughts running through your brain. Connections are made, concepts are formed, words are attached – and words trigger pictures that trigger emotions. The output of all this activity is thoughts which are continually building on other thoughts to form beliefs. The critical point is that you self-regulate to your belief level. Believe peace is possible and you will elevate your thinking to the possibility.

If you believe peace is impossible, your mind will regulate to that belief. Why not believe peace IS possible?

> *Ron: I grew up during the height of the Cold War and the nuclear arms race, so mistrust of communism was part of my childhood conditioning. Russia, China, Cuba – they were our enemies; no two ways about it. As an adult, I didn't give much thought to how deeply rooted this mistrust was until an experience at West Point Military Academy brought it home. I was a guest on campus and was exploring on my own when I ran smack into a group of Chinese military people. They were wearing those distinctive uniforms and hats with the red star. I was stunned. What the heck were these communist Chinese*

people doing at our preeminent military academy? I asked around and learned that they were part of a military exchange program, but talk about disorienting! I had come face-to-face with my own deeply buried barriers to coexistence. It was a mind-opening experience. Ironically, 25 years later I am married to a southeast Asian woman of Chinese ancestry.

In order to have world peace, you need to believe world peace is possible, or at least that you can peacefully coexist with others in the same place at the same time, despite your differences. Once you believe that, you begin to unleash the potential of your mind.

Start by examining your beliefs and seeing which "truths" are not serving you well. Where did they come from? Trace them back as far as you can. Where did you learn your beliefs about other cultures, other genders, other religions? Was it from parents, teachers or friends; was it a bad experience; was it the media? So many of our beliefs have their roots in what we were taught early in our lives, or what is fed to us in media soundbites. If we never challenge these beliefs, we limit our potential to grow.

The next time you feel challenged to coexist, do a self-diagnostic in the name of peace. Explore the beliefs behind your feelings. Are they serving you well or is it time to change? The point of this self-examination is not to strip away your truths or undermine your beliefs. The point is to motivate you to more closely examine what your beliefs are, what factual basis they have and whether they are serving the cause of peace.

FIGHT FOR PEACE?

In developing our seven principles of peace, we have discovered the importance of language and the need for thoughtfulness in the language we use.

Gregg: On a visit to Ireland, my wife Sandra and I were sharing a pub meal with a new friend. We got talking about the "Troubles" in Northern Ireland and how hopeful people are for a lasting peace. I said something about people fighting for peace. It's a common phrase: you fight for your rights, you fight for what you believe in, you fight for peace. Helen laughed and said, "Hah, there's an oxymoron if ever I've heard one. How can you fight for peace?" She questioned whether fighting for peace was actually part of the problem. It was one of those moments when you suddenly see something you've taken for granted in a completely different light. Of course you can't fight for peace, and too many people do. So where does that leave us? For Helen, it meant thinking about peace in a different way, a way that did not involve fighting. But if we do not fight for peace, what then?

SURRENDER TO PEACE?

If you cannot fight for peace, can you surrender to peace? It is an unsettling thought, but before we go any further, let's define "surrender". We are not talking about giving up your beliefs or giving in to the power of another. We are talking about giving yourself to a cause you believe in.

> "Thoughts of surrender are so freighted with military connotation that is requires conscious effort to notice that surrender can mean a whole hearted giving of oneself – to a cause, or in friendship and love."
> - Huston Smith, The World's Religions

Surrendering does not sit well, especially with men. Men do not like to surrender anything to anyone. We are not suggesting that you surrender to the authority of someone else's idea. Instead, we are asking you to consider surrendering to a *better* idea or being open to the possibility that a different idea might have value. It is not easy. Look at Colin Powell's reaction to Mikhail Gorbachev and disarmament. Gorbachev was taking bold steps toward ending the Cold War. Despite skepticism and deeply rooted distrust on both sides, he persevered and the U.S.S.R. and U.S.A. were able to move away from a policy of mutually assured destruction (aptly nicknamed MAD) toward coexistence. In effect, decision-makers in both countries surrendered, reluctantly, even grudgingly, to a better idea – peaceful coexistence.

OR RELAX INTO PEACE?

Ron: I realize people struggle with the whole idea of surrendering to peace. One experience makes me wonder if what we're actually doing is relaxing into peace. It happened on my way home from work. I stopped to get a soft drink at the 7-Eleven® down the road. As I was walking out the door, an argument erupted between an African American customer and an East Indian clerk. I was already out the door when I thought, "Maybe I can help make peace." It was like coexistence rose up inside me. Then I thought, "Wait a minute, people get killed doing stuff like that!" In an instant, fear rose up inside. It froze me, but I was thinking and as I'm thinking, I glance around the parking lot and notice the only other car has a car seat with a baby in the back. That decided it for me: if the customer was a dad, it was safe enough. I walked back inside and the two guys were really going at it. I asked if I could help. It turns out the customer was trying to return a container of ice milk and get ice cream instead – there is a difference. The clerk was calling his boss to see if it was okay. I offered to pay the difference but the minute I reached into my pocket they stopped arguing and said not to worry about it. I'm not sure if they surrendered to peace or just relaxed into it. Back outside, I thought, "Hey, that was a peace project!" It may have been a tempest in a teapot, but for me, it was détente on a neighborhood level.

A lot of things happen to push us to decisions. In the 7-Eleven® story, ethnicity played a role, the baby in the car seat played a role, past conditioning played a role; but Ron's belief in coexistence trumped all other beliefs and he acted according to his belief.

TO CHANGE YOUR BELIEF, UNDERSTAND HOW YOUR MIND WORKS

You already know that you act in accordance with the truth as you believe and perceive it to be, and that your thoughts become your beliefs. In order to change your beliefs, you need to know how your mind works. Cognitive theory can help you move toward peace because it can help you understand how your mind works. You can begin to recognize the thought processes behind challenges to coexistence. This is important; remember, peace begins in your own mind and then works its way out into your life.

Cognitive theory breaks your inner thought process down into three parts: conscious, subconscious and creative subconscious. When you meet someone whose religious beliefs, for example, challenge your ability to coexist, your mind is busy in all three areas. Your conscious mind is evaluating the person based on your truths, realities and attitudes. These are stored in your subconscious, and they are based on information provided to you by others – teachers, parents, family, friends, media, a friend of a friend of a friend, YouTube. Once information is stored in your subconscious as "truth", it is upheld by the guard dogs of your creative subconscious.

A main role of your creative subconscious is to protect your sanity, something it will do at all costs – even at the cost of truth. As far as your mind is concerned, **sanity is more important than success**[3].

This is something we will return to in Principle 6: Adventure is Our Friend. This relationship between subconscious and creative subconscious is what hypnotists temporarily tap into when they get willing audience members to do outrageous things, such as barking like a dog or struggling to lift a feather. The thing to keep in mind is that when you are faced with a coexistence situation, you adjudicate not on the evidence before your eyes, but on the whole range of your past experience and conditioning.

HOW YOUR MIND WORKS: A MODEL[4]

Understanding how your mind works is core to understanding coexistence. At any given moment, make that every given moment, your conscious mind is busy perceiving, associating, evaluating and deciding or adjudicating. Your subconscious mind stores all this information as your realities, truths, habits, attitudes and self-image. Your creative subconscious maintains your sanity (meaning your reality), solves conflicts and creates energy, based on information stored in the subconscious.

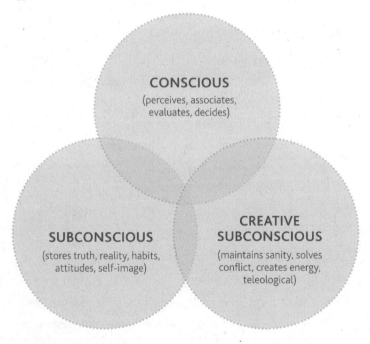

A powerful example of the connection between understanding how the mind works and coexistence can be found in inner city Los Angeles. During the summer, neighborhood parks in an area of South LA had turned into magnets for gang violence. Then in 2008, a program called Summer Night Lights was introduced. The goal was to create a détente between rival gangs by recruiting neighborhood kids, gang members included, to help keep the peace in parks. As part of the program, the kids underwent an intensive week of The Pacific Institute's PX2® education. This included education on how the mind works and how beliefs shape expectations, as well as tools for taking control of the way they think and use that power to change the way they live their lives. In the first year of the program, crime in local parks dropped dramatically and the area reported its lowest crime rate since 1967. This success led to the program's repetition the following year, this time with private funding. Summer Night Lights proved that even if rival gangs with a history of violence could not surrender to peace, they could, and did, take advantage of an opportunity to coexist. They relaxed into peace, but it required a bigger, better idea to convince them – and that idea was that peaceful coexistence was possible.

> Coexistence begins at a "thought" level. When faced with a new idea or belief, your mind evaluates based on information stored in your subconscious – information that might or might not be accurate. Based on this evaluation, your creative subconscious will make sure you behave in accordance with your belief. Coexistence starts inside and works its way into your life, your community, your world.

COEXISTENCE AND EGO IDENTITY

If you have ever wondered why differences – personal, racial, religious, economic, social, cultural – challenge our ability to coexist, Erik Erikson's theory of psychosocial development is a good starting point for understanding. In a nutshell, Erikson[5] maintains that personality develops in stages throughout life, not just when you are young. You move through distinct stages at distinct points, and each stage represents a growth process. Either skills are acquired and you develop a sense of accomplishment, or skills are not acquired and you end up feeling inadequate.

The journey begins in infancy, when you learn to trust or mistrust. During your childhood you learn autonomy, initiative and industry or you learn shame, doubt, guilt and inferiority. In your teen and young adult years, you grapple with ego identity versus confusion and intimacy versus isolation. The journey does not end there: you continue to build on these early lessons throughout your life. If you have a good sense of your own identity, you have a much better chance of mastering the later stages: generativity (concern for people outside of self and family) and integrity (acceptance of self and sense of others).

Erikson's theory is fascinating in its own right, and there are books on ego identity you can read if you want to know more. We introduce the concept here to illustrate the role your sense of identity plays in coexistence. You need to build a strong sense of self, a strong ego identity, in order to practice coexistence and world peace. The Dalai Lama is a high-level example. He is a man who has figured out his identity and it shows in his ability to model intimacy, generativity and integrity – the mature stages of ego identity. Yet he describes himself as a simple Buddhist monk. People often smile when he says this, because they think he is being modest; in fact, he is being serious. He will tell you that if he regards himself as anything more than a simple Buddhist monk, there is a risk he will put himself on a different level than other people and become "too important". His statement of identity is not self-effacing; it is affirmative. He maintains his identity by monitoring his self-talk and disputing when other people try to tell him otherwise – these are tools we'll talk about in Principle 3: Diversity Is Our Strength.

People who struggle with ego identity are more prone to confusion, isolation, stagnation and despair. These are dangerous waters. It is hard to be accepting of others when you are not sure of your own value. Other people's differences make you feel insecure. In order to feel right about yourself, you need to make the other person wrong. Emotions can get so turbulent you cross over into dehumanizing anyone who doesn't look, talk, behave or believe like you. And when you dehumanize another person or another country, peace gives way to conflict and violence. How many times have we seen news stories about people who say, when asked why they have committed a violent crime, "I didn't think of them [the other person] as human."

While writing this book, we came across a news story about a father who allegedly drowned his three teenage daughters because he was upset about their behavior. Somehow, he crossed a line that took him all the way from "I don't agree with how you are behaving" to "I don't want you to exist". His actions enabled him to maintain his stringent belief system, but at what cost? This is the absolute opposite of coexistence, and the first step down this road is easier than you might think.

LABELING: THE FIRST ACT OF VIOLENCE

What picture does "infidel dog" conjure up in your mind? How about "bleeding heart liberal"? Who do you think of? Is your reaction positive or negative? Putting a label on someone is often described as the first act of violence. Negative labels turn people into one-dimensional stereotypes; they dehumanize. We all do it; we need to learn to catch ourselves in the act. Instead of labeling, try seeing the whole person. Try to be curious about the different points of view: why do those people think that, feel that, say that? What is at the root of those viewpoints?

The media is one of the biggest perpetrators of labels. Modern media thrives on controversy. The problem is that the debate is rarely even-handed. Instead, it is a clash of polarized opinions and a contest of wills to have one opinion triumph over all others. Choosing which side of a polarized debate you are on is not the road to coexistence, and certainly not the way to world peace. Coexistence demands that you be able to see more than your own perspective. It challenges you to see the shades of grey and contrasting points of view. It also throws out the ultimate challenge: even when you do not agree with other ideas, can you live peacefully alongside them? Test yourself: pick an issue you feel strongly about – now argue the other side. If the thought fills you with revulsion, pick a different issue, one with fewer emotional overtones. Be honest about developing your argument for the other side. The point of the exercise is not to change your mind or your opinions; it is simply a way to help you coexistence with different points of view.

> *Ron: My dad always taught us that there were two sides to every argument. I was lucky to have that reinforced at school. I was an athlete but I was also in the debate club. In debate club, you had to research both sides of an issue because you didn't know until the last minute if you were arguing pro or con, so you had to be able to argue both sides of the issue. That's where I learned that two opposing ideas can coexist in the same room. It was great training for citizenship.*

BREAKING FREE OF HISTORY

Whether in politics or religion, in South LA or in your own community, world peace is the bigger, better idea. Coexistence is the way to get there. It is an opportunity to break free from your conditioning and to look at the world in a new way. Believing in world peace is the first step in peaceful coexistence. In the next chapter, Blindness Is Our Problem, we will talk about overcoming the barrier of blindness and the scary possibility that everyone might just be partially right.

REFLECTIVE QUESTIONS

- When did you last surrender? To what?
- Who do you coexist well with?
- Who don't you coexist well with?
- Where have you found a way to coexist and who with?
- Think of an instance when you did or did not coexist – what were some of the characteristics of the experience?
- What beliefs do you hold that are not helping you?
- What are the labels you use, especially the ones you're not so proud of?
- Do you have any peace or coexistence projects? What are they?

Men in the game are blind to what men looking on can see.
Chinese Proverb

PRINCIPLE 2: BLINDNESS IS OUR PROBLEM

In this chapter, we dig deeper into how the mind works to reveal the tricks and traps undermining your ability to peacefully coexist with other ideas, other cultures, other beliefs. It is all about identifying and challenging your blind spots.

Accepting that other people have opinions, beliefs and even truths different than your own is necessary for peaceful coexistence. It sounds easy enough, except that your mind creates barriers. When other beliefs do not match your own, your mind can build blind spots to the possibility that these other beliefs might be valid. Recognizing that blindness is our problem is the second principle of **World Peace, Really!**.

> *Gregg: I love TED – it's a website that has some really fascinating video talks by all kinds of people. One day I was listening to a Nigerian writer named Chimamanda Ngozi Adichie[6]. The title of her talk got my attention: "The Danger of the Single Story."*

It's about how one-sided stories about people and countries can lead to long-term misunderstanding. Chimamanda uses her own life experiences to illustrate her point. For example, she says she grew up reading American and British children's books and didn't realize until much later that girls like her, "girls with skin the color of chocolate", could exist in literature. As a middle-class child, she remembers feeling enormous pity for her family's houseboy so she was amazed to discover that he had a family life and that his mother made beautiful baskets. Her single story of the houseboy had been his poverty. At university in the U.S., she remembers her American roommate's shock at hearing Chimamanda came from a middle class African family. Her roommate's single story of Africa was one of poverty and catastrophe. As I listened to these single stories, it confirmed in my mind that blindness really is our problem.

Worth a look – TED says it is a nonprofit devoted to "ideas worth spreading". It started as a conference for people in technology, entertainment and design. Now, it's a global treasure chest of ideas. You can watch TedTalks on just about every topic under the sun – books, music, science, religion, the environment, space, philosophy, and a lot more. www.ted.com

YOUR PERCEPTION OF TRUTH

The damage we do when we limit ourselves to single stories is that we treat them as truth. Do you have a single story about Iran, Israel, China, Russia, Darfur, Haiti? How about closer to home, do you have a single story about your neighbors in the U.S., Canada or Mexico? What is your single story – try writing it down. How does it look on paper? The thing about your truth is that it is not everyone's truth. There can be no single truth for the world's 6.6 billion people, not when truth is based on individual perceptions, which in turn are based on conditioning and experience.

Fear is a powerful conditioning experience, so is anger. Imagine you are a gifted athlete with a chance of making your national Olympic Team. You sacrifice everything for your dream: you put school on hold, career on hold, family on hold. And you succeed – you make the team. Then politics intervenes and your dream comes crashing down. It happened to many athletes in 1980 when most Western nations boycotted the Summer Games in Moscow. It happened again in 1984 when Soviet-bloc countries boycotted the 1984 Summer Games in Los Angeles. Do you think such an experience could provide the foundation for a life-long political affiliation? You bet it could. Many of our beliefs are based on experiences that made us really, really angry … or really, really scared, sad, happy and so on. This is another function of how your mind works, and it is called locking-on and locking-out[7].

When you limit your perception of other possibilities, you are locking-on to a single story, opinion or viewpoint, and locking-out all the other possibilities. Lock-on, lock-out leaves you with a restricted view of alternatives. Locking-on to an opinion or attitude locks-out opposing or different information. It is a defense mechanism that helps us to survive, but it also works against us when change and flexibility are needed. We use a well-known visual aid in our workshops to help people break the log jam of their beliefs. You might have seen it before: it is a drawing of a young lady, or perhaps you see an old lady. It depends on your perspective. This optical illusion shows lock-on, lock-out in action. Who do you see in the drawing, the young lady or old lady? Can you see the other image?

Ron: After the 2008 Summer Olympics, I was part of TPI team working with the U.S. National Swim Team. These are the 100 best swimmers in the country. They're disciplined, dedicated and absolutely focused – so at first I was surprised at the trouble they had seeing both images when we introduced the drawing. A lot of them really locked onto the first image they saw. They just couldn't see the other lady. You almost needed a hammer and chisel to unlock them. I realized that their ability to focus, which is such an important part of being a high performance athlete, has a consequence in that it can make it harder to unlock from your truth. This made me think, what about the rest of us, what about me? What am I locked on to?

Blindness is your problem when you lock onto a truth and then need a hammer and chisel to free yourself to see another point of view.

DISARMING YOUR MIND

Gregg: I am often surprised at the things I lock onto. When some friends and I were building a property in Mexico that had access to several golf courses, people kept asking if I was looking forward to golfing there. Most people who know me know that I love to golf. But my knee-jerk response was, "I'll never golf in Mexico." Why did I say that? I'm not sure, but I had a sudden flashback of my dad saying "no" to things without even thinking about them. That's what I was doing. I had locked on to a knee-jerk response as if it was a deeply-held truth. What makes this more interesting is that I defended my point of view even though I didn't know why I thought that way. I didn't want to look stupid. Lucky for me, I had friends who were willing to challenge me on it. That and the fact that I really do love to golf won out over my embarrassment at having to back down. I busted through my blindness. Why wouldn't I golf in Mexico? I love golfing in Mexico!

Locking-on and locking-out can interfere with your ability to peacefully coexist. You have to challenge your ideas and beliefs, or be challenged on them, in order to see where you have locked out other ideas and beliefs. We call this disarming your mind. Here's another exercise we use to help people unlock.

Read the following sentence:

> Finished files are the result
> of years of scientific
> study combined with
> the experience of many years.

How many F's can you find – three, four, five? If you got six, congratulations. There is no trick, and yet most people do not see all the F's. Why? Because most of us learn to read phonetically, so when we see the word "of" we hear the word "ov" – the "f" becomes "v".

Doing the F card exercise has two immediate benefits. First, it creates open-mindedness. **You might be missing something**. None of us likes to admit we have blind spots, but this is an easy way to demonstrate that, in fact, we do have them; it is just the way the mind works. Second, everything we hold to be true is framed by our past conditioning. This means that your experiences, combined with how you were raised, taught and coached (such as learning to read phonetically), impact your ability to perceive reality.

DO YOU HAVE SCOTOMAS?

If you positively know something to be 100 percent true, you positively have a scotoma. A scotoma is a blindspot, an area of impaired vision within your normal field of vision. When used in relation to how you think, it is a sensory locking-out of information from your environment, particularly other truths that do not match your perception of truth. Scotomas prevent you from seeing alternatives. Remember your creative subconscious? If your past conditioning (which has framed your truth) does not match what you perceive, your creative subconscious will protect your sanity (your truth) by blocking out other possibilities. To your creative subconscious, your sanity is more important than reality.

When you are no longer 100 percent certain of what you were certain of before, it is easier to acknowledge your scotomas. You allow the possibility that you might be missing something. Once that door is pushed open, you create the opportunity for new learning. You no longer have to defend your ideas as right or label other ideas as wrong.

Before we move on, let's add an important qualifier: recognizing the validity of other ideas does not mean you have to agree with them, nor does it require you to abandon beliefs you feel strongly about. Instead, recognizing that you have scotomas can help you find ways to peacefully coexist with other ideas, other religious beliefs, other cultural practices. It is a way to disarm your mind. You can begin to relax into peace by accepting that there might be more than one way to look at an issue, more to the "other side" than you are allowing yourself to see. By lowering your defenses, you open your mind to coexistence. In our workshops, we ask for a show of hands after the F card exercise. Who has a scotoma? Most everyone puts up their hand, and anyone that doesn't is usually teased about having a scotoma about having a scotoma. Once you declare that what you see or believe may not be totally true, you are ready to move forward.

> Once you know that you don't know, you open the door to other possibilities. Your truth may not, in fact, be the whole truth. The moral of the story: in your perception of truth, is it possible you are missing something?

YOUR PLACE IN THE "KOSMOS"

If we are to coexist, to have world peace, each of us needs to understand that while my worldview is the truth for me, other worldviews are equally true for other people. It is a tough sell. There are so many issues we feel strongly about: the war on terror, the debate on health care, the issue of gay marriage. Can people on opposite sides of such issues really coexist? Recognizing your single stories, lock-on/lock-out and scotomas is a start. A school of thought called integral theory also puts forward ideas you can use to move toward peaceful coexistence.

Integral theory explores the human condition using an integrated framework of psychological, social and spiritual insights. We are not going to discuss the theory in detail here, but we do want to introduce several relevant concepts. The first is the notion of a Kosmic (yes, with a "k") address. The idea comes from Ken Wilbur[8], one of the best known integral theorists. He suggests that every individual has a unique Kosmic address, and that this address represents your view of the world. The tricky thing is that it is not a static; your Kosmic address is in a constant state of flux. Where you are today is a little different than where you were yesterday and it will be a little different again tomorrow, because you are constantly evolving. We tend to forget this. We arrive at adulthood and figure that's it, the evolution is over. But as Erikson's theory of ego identity illustrated in Principle 1, this is not the case. Personal development is a life-long process. This means your Kosmic address is in flux because you are in flux. You are constantly in motion as a developing human being – your Kosmic address represents the sum total of you, at any given moment.

Your Kosmic address is meant to be dynamic. You get into trouble when you do not allow change to happen, when you think your Kosmic address should be static. In order to stay the same, you have to build a lot of scotomas about the world around you. This causes your perspective to become fixed. You lock on to your beliefs and lock out different beliefs. You build barriers to peaceful coexistence. Blindness becomes your problem.

....

> Your Kosmic address represents you, in total, at any given moment. It is neither wrong nor right; it is simply where you are at this point in time.

....

THE SCARY POSSIBILITIES OF PARTIALLY RIGHT

Another integral concept – and a challenging one – is that every school of thought is only partially right. Instead of one "correct" worldview, for example, there is validity in many worldviews. If you follow this line of thinking, then no single philosophy, religion, political theory or lifestyle is the "true" one. All are valid but at best only partially right. This means some of the finest thinkers our world has ever known – Aristotle, Confucius, Moses, Muhammad, Siddhartha, Jesus – were only partially right.

Whoa! Did your mind just slam on the brakes? Before you toss our book out the window, understand that we are talking about interpretation, not faith. Let's say that again, we are talking about interpretation, not faith. Faith is a deeply personal, deeply emotional issue. Interpretation of faith is something separate. There are different sects within every major world religion: Christianity, Islam, Judaism, Hinduism and Buddhism. Who decides which is the right one? Is it right for one interpretation to dominate? Do we all need to agree on one religion, one practice? What happens to those who have a different interpretation?

So often, it is interpretation of faith that plunges nations and neighbors into conflict. This is where the tension and strain begin, as one jostles for dominance over another. But is it really possible that only one is the right one? Wilber offers a different point of view: "The fact is, all of the various theories, practices, and established paradigms—in the sciences, arts, and humanities—are already being practiced: they are already arising in a Kosmos that clearly allows them to arise, and the question is not, which of those is the correct one, but what is the structure of the Kosmos such that it allows all of those to arise in the first place? What is the architecture of a universe that includes so many wonderful rooms?"[9]

In our mind, it makes much more sense that different interpretations of faith can each be partially right. Ah, but if nothing is completely true, then is anything true? Are we suggesting another version of relativism? No. The usefulness of "partially right" is that it illustrates how our beliefs can create scotomas that prevent us from seeing the validity of other points of view. "Partially right" opens the door to seeing past our scotomas and allowing coexistence.

> Faith often gets slammed for being at the root of human conflict, but it is interpretations of faith that cause the rifts between us.

Being partially right is an uneasy feeling. There is more comfort, more ego gratification in certainty. Human beings like certainty; we like absolute truths. This takes us back to something we discussed earlier: *you act in accordance with the truth as you believe and perceive it to be.* World peace demands that we open our eyes to other truths and to do that, we must recognize how our perception of truth creates blind spots within us. If you believe you are completely right, then anyone who believes differently becomes wrong. The world begins to separate into us and them, enemy and ally. That is not a path to coexistence.

CREATING HEROES AND VILLAINS

> *Gregg: Life was easier before Ron introduced me to this annoying concept of partially right. It's uncomfortable. It forces me to surrender my strongly held and really enjoyable beliefs. One of them is of shining knight Barack Obama and evil empire George Bush. Like a lot of people outside the U.S., I think my view of President Bush was overtly negative and my*

view of President Obama was overtly positive. The easy image of good versus bad appealed to me. I didn't want to hear any information that might mess that up, like suggesting President Obama is only partially right ... or that President Bush could be partially right. It's a really uncomfortable idea for me, but it keeps popping up. When Bush was in my hometown on a speaking engagement last year, I debated whether or not to go. In the end I couldn't get myself to buy a ticket, but I was embarrassed because I also didn't join the peaceful protest in front of the event centre. I should have gone and heard him, or I should have been out marching; instead I was stuck in neutral. Was I coexisting, I don't think so. I was simply stuck. It didn't feel too good. And dang it, if Bush didn't get a standing ovation. Growing up is so hard.

Human beings have a tendency to be monological. That is, we tend to believe that our personal worldview, religion, culture or whatever is the right one. It is fair to say that we are partially right, because our worldview represents our truth, based on our experience and learning. But our truth may not be your truth; in fact, there is a high probability it will not be your truth. That's the trouble with monological thinking; it is continually coming into conflict with other, equally "right" worldviews.

We all have heroes and villains. But in a world view, is it possible that our heroes and villains are only partially right?

Monological thinking can set neighbor against neighbor, race against race, religion against religion. It can also push us toward labeling. In Coexistence Is Our Goal, we talked about how pinning a label on an individual or group is often the first act of violence. Labels not only demonize and dehumanize, they create scotomas. In 2002, when President Bush called North Korea, Iraq and Iran the "axis of evil," he attached a negative label to those countries that will long outlive his presidency. He also created a collective scotoma in the U.S. and elsewhere, so that it is hard to see anything but the bad side of Iran, Iraq or North Korea. Yet there is good in those countries. It is a lesson in how our leaders can generate collective blindness simply by the language they use.

> Monological thinking tells us that our personal worldview is the right one. Trouble is, it sets us up for conflict with different monological worldviews.

President Bush was reacting to a specific set of information in his speech. In 2009, President Obama showed a different tactic when he reached out to the Muslim world during a speech in Egypt. His approach was based on respect and inclusiveness. Was one right and one wrong? You will find people who passionately believe in the rightness of Bush's speech and those who passionately believe in the rightness of Obama's speech. More often than not, you will also find them in conflict with each other. Blindness sets in when you become convinced of the rightness of your point of view or belief.

When we talk about blindness as our problem, we are not talking about right or wrong – we are talking about creating open-mindedness and a climate for coexistence. Even as we are saying this, we are aware of the pitfalls inherent in our own passion for peace. If we become too convinced of our own ideas, too evangelical, we will set the stage for a whole new set of scotomas. Applying the concept of "partially right" provides an effective check to our zeal. It cautions us that, even with all our passionate belief, there are other, equally valid truths we may not see.

> *Ron: I think another way to look at partially right is to think of the world as a map of polka dots. The dots are all different colors and sizes. There are lots of areas where the dots overlap, but there is also a lot separation: we live in our own dots. I got a taste of this on a trip to Saudi Arabia to participate in some seminars. I knew I was going into a very different culture and I knew there were things about that culture I didn't agree with. It really bothered me to see women segregated to seats at the back of a bus and to see a woman switched by a man because her arms were showing. I felt passionate rightness about my response to treatment of women. But I also saw good things in that culture. For example, I was visiting the market one day and the call to prayer sounded. Everything shut down; it literally went from a crowded, noisy market to silence. The entire society stops what it's doing five times a day to pray. That's impressive. How do I reconcile those two examples? I don't know that I can, but I can coexist with them. It isn't comfortable, but recognizing that I am only partially right never is. There is no easy answer.*

BLIND SPOTS IMPACT WORLD PEACE

We build blind spots to many things that we might not connect to world peace or coexistence, and yet they do connect, forcibly. Poverty, hunger, education, gender equality, health care, environmental sustainability, development – the United Nations has singled these issues out in its millennial goals because they lie at the root of social and political unrest.

Would you argue against eradicating hunger or poverty? Probably not, but do you think you have scotomas about either issue? Before you answer, remember that **if you positively know something, you positively have a scotoma**[10]. Think about it. How much do you know about poverty in your community? How many people use the local Food Bank? How about education – what is the high school drop-out rate or the truancy rate among elementary school kids? These kinds of issues might not be part of your everyday reality, so you might develop blind spots to them. Yet research continues to show that poverty, hunger, poor health and lack of education can pose serious stumbling blocks to coexistence – not just in poor, undeveloped countries but in our own communities. Sometimes, it takes a dramatic event to see the reality.

> *Gregg: My wife used to teach at an inner city school. She would tell me stories about young children whose basic food, shelter and safety needs were not being met. It was shocking to realize this was happening in our own community. One day, I saw it happening right on my doorstep. I came home after work to find Sandra standing on our porch with a 12-year-old girl, who was clinging to her 5-year old sister. Both girls were crying and a social worker was literally pulling the 5-year-old out of her sister's arms. The older girl had reported abuse at home and was being put in protective custody, but the 5-year-old was being returned to the home. Having this unfold on our doorstep was something neither Sandra nor I will ever forget; our scotomas were ripped away. Because of that, I was motivated to do something and the next day at work, we started a community project to provide role models for inner city kids and to raise money for programs that provided food and shelter. But I couldn't do those things until I busted through my scotomas; blindness was my problem.*

... AND INNER PEACE

Blindness not only impacts the way we behave, it impacts the way we feel about ourselves and our place in the world. When Ron encountered the customer and clerk arguing in the 7-Eleven®, his decision to get involved only came after he had left the store and seen the child in the car seat. Gregg's decision to lead a community project at his workplace only came after a drama played out on his doorstep. Uncovering blind spots can be painful in other ways.

> *Ron: A while ago, I underwent a personal leadership review at work. I remember opening the results of my survey, reading for a few minutes, then slamming it shut. I've never been comfortable asking other people how I can be better, and this time I sure didn't like the answer I got. My first thought was, those jerks! I literally felt lightheaded. My instructor just kept telling me to relax and hang with it. I was still disoriented that night. When I told my wife, she said, bless her heart, "Those jerks!" By the next morning I had had time to assimilate it. As uncomfortable as it was, it also highlighted some of my scotomas about myself, and that gave me something to focus on. When I got back to the office, my colleagues said right away there was something different about me. I had already written several affirmations and was starting to turn the whole scotoma-busting thing into a good learning experience, but man, it was painful.*

Ron's story is similar to what happens in a coming-of-age story in which childhood perspectives are blasted apart by disillusionment. What do you mean there is no Santa Claus? This process continues into our adult life. Disillusionment, accompanied by periodic busting of scotomas, actually becomes an important part of learning. It is not comfortable, but it is essential to growth.

SCOTOMA-BUSTING

Recognizing our blind spots can be a liberating experience. The liberation may come with some pain. Tell yourself it is a good pain. It puts emotional force behind your will to change. Unless you have that emotional connection, you might remain blind to your own scotomas. The process of scotoma-busting begins by recognizing that you have them. Everyone with scotomas, raise your hand. Good for you! That's your first breakthrough ... and another step toward world peace.

REFLECTIVE QUESTIONS

- How would you define faith? Interpretation?
- Can your faith/interpretation coexist with someone else?
- How did your opinions about other people form? Are your sources reliable?
- Do you really know the truth about people halfway around the world who you've never met? How do you explain this?
- What are your truths?
- What are you absolutely sure of?
- Do you get angry defending your truth? What happens when you do?
- What scares you about other people? Do you really know?
- Are you confident enough to coexist with a different truth than your own?
- List 3 truths that always seem to get you into trouble with other people.
- List 5 truths that you share with your best friends.

"We may have different religions, different languages, different colored skin, but we all belong to one human race."
Kofi Annan, Secretary General of the United Nations, 1997-2006

PRINCIPLE 3:
DIVERSITY IS OUR STRENGTH

In this chapter, you'll challenge your comfort zones, discover the difference between dialogue and discussion and learn to dispute information fed to you about "other" ideas, people, cultures and beliefs. It is all part of practicing diversity, an essential principle in world peace.

On the road to world peace, diversity is our strength. The power of diversity is that it challenges our comfortable stereotypes about "us" and "them." It is both wonderful and frightening. It takes us out of our comfort zone into uncharted territory. While there are many facets to diversity, two of the most contentious are race and religion.

Do you feel society has made progress in relations between black and white? Was the election of the first African American president a major breakthrough? In an interview after Barack Obama's election, with comedian Chris Rock[11] was asked similar questions.

His response was interesting. "When you say progress, you're acting like what happened before wasn't crazy. It's like, oh, we've made a lot of progress and there's no more segregation. Segregation is retarded. It's crazy to think you're better than somebody ... that's insane."

What about religion? Do you believe Christians, Jews and Muslims are making progress in learning to coexist peacefully, in the same place, at the same time? It is a question "three interfaith amigos" Rabbi Ted Falcon, Pastor Don Mackenzie and Sheikh Jamal Rahman ask in their book, *Getting to the Heart of Interfaith: The Eye-opening, Hope-filled Friendship of a Pastor, a Rabbi and a Sheikh*[12]. An important part of the book is their individual declaration of what core teaching they value most about their tradition. "Oneness," says Rabbi Ted. "Unconditional love," says Pastor Don. "Compassion," says Sheikh Jamal. They follow this with something even more courageous – they declare what they believe to be the "untruths" in their own faith. Rabbi Ted points to the notion that Jews are the chosen people. Pastor Don identifies the idea that Christianity is the only way to God. Sheikh Jamal says it is the "sword" verses in the Koran, like "kill the unbeliever".

These are just examples of the kind of dialogue happening on diversity issues. Diversity can also refer to language, politics and philosophy. It might refer to different schools of economic thought, such as free market, closed market or regulated market. It might refer to different forms of government: democratic republic, parliamentary democracy, communism, sultanate, monarchy, oligarchy. Diversity might even refer to the subject line on the billions of internet searches conducted every month. It underlines a point we made in Principle 2: Blindness is Our Problem: there is no single truth for all 6.6 billion of us who share Planet Earth. Each of us has our own truth, and that makes for an incredible range of diversity.

THE WORLD IS CONVERGING ... ON OUR DOORSTEP

We believe the world is moving toward coexistence. If you want to know what that looks like, check out Hans Rosling[13] on TED. His presentations are scotoma-busting. For those of us raised on a single story of the Third World (i.e. poverty) it comes as a surprise to see that the trajectory toward health and prosperity is the same as in the West. Are there discrepancies? Absolutely – there are crisis areas, but the overall path is upward. The gap between "us" and "them" is disappearing.

We also believe there is a fork in the road ahead. Many of the challenges we face are completely new. The world is interconnected in ways few of us ever imagined. There are more of us than at any other point in history. We can travel just about anywhere, trade just about anything and communicate all kinds of information in the blink of an eye. The combined energy and ambition of the world's growing population is putting enormous pressure on our environment. These trends are straining our ability to live in peace with our environment and our neighbors.

Across North America, immigration on a scale not seen since the early 1900s is changing the face of Main Street. Immigrants are coming from more than 200 different countries around the world, and they are bringing with them their languages, cultural traditions and belief systems. How do you coexist with people who not only look different than you, but think differently, pray differently, *believe* differently? Diversity scares us. It tests our sense of self. If you have not developed a strong sense of your own ego identity, you will feel the need to protect yourself from people, ideas and beliefs that challenge your worldview.

IS THE WORLD BECOMING MORE OR LESS TOLERANT?

If you go by what you see on the nightly news, you might think the world is becoming less tolerant of diversity. But the images presented by the media represent a single story – the "news" that stands out from all the other events. In 2009, Gallup released a Coexist Index to measure attitudes in Europe and North America toward religious faiths different from our own. The survey is one barometer of our acceptance of diversity. Based on responses, Gallup classifies national populations as:

- *Isolated*: individuals tend not to be members of any particular faith group, but if they are, they tend to believe in the truth of their perspective above all others and do not want to know about other religions. They neither respect nor feel respected by other faiths.

- *Tolerant*: individuals have a "live-and-let-live" attitude toward people of other faiths and generally feel that they treat others of different faiths with respect. They are not likely to learn from or about other religions.

- *Integrated*: individuals actively seek to know more about and learn from different religious traditions. They believe most faiths make a positive contribution to society. They not only respect people from other faith traditions, but they also feel respected by them.

At present, the attitude of most people in Europe and North America is either integrated or tolerant of other religions. The figures to watch over the coming years are the Isolated and Integrated categories. An increase in the percentage of Isolated could indicate a population moving toward conflict, while an increase in Integrated could indicate a move toward peaceful coexistence.

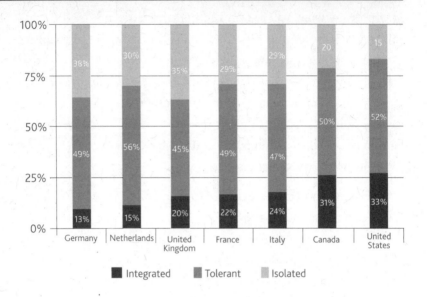

Source: *The Gallup Coexist Index 2009: A Global Study of Interfaith Relations*, www.muslimwestfacts.com/mwf/118249/Gallup-Coexist-Index-2009.aspx

CHALLENGE YOUR COMFORT ZONE

Gregg: I remember going out for dinner with some gay friends. An older woman they knew came up to the table to say hello. In an open, laughing way she said something like, "It looks pretty gay out tonight." I immediately wanted to stand up and say, "No, no, I'm straight!" I was way out of my comfort zone, even though they were friends of mine. Reflecting on it later I thought, what if I didn't have those friends or didn't put myself into new situations? My life would be less rich.

Ron: I've talked about my visit to Saudi Arabia, but I'm going to go back there because it was an experience that absolutely challenged my comfort zone. I remember one evening when I sat down with a senior member of the sponsoring company, who was Muslim. He said he had listened to me for two days, now

> it was my turn to listen to him. For 45 minutes, he shared the teachings of his religion with me. I'm probably as committed to my Christian faith as he is to his Muslim faith, and I thought, oh boy, are we going to get into an argument over religion? I was uncomfortable at first, but I just relaxed into it. I listened and learned, and I wasn't uncomfortable anymore.

Will you abandon your faith and convert to another if someone talks to you about their religion. Will you turn gay if you go out for dinner with homosexual friends? Will something bad happen if you listen to an opposing political view? Before we can acknowledge that diversity is our strength, we have to get comfortable with it and that's tougher than it sounds. Human beings have well-defined comfort zones: limited, defined physical or psychological areas in which you feel at ease. We are conditioned from childhood to avoid diversity and stick to our comfort zones. Just as you might go out of your way to avoid conflict by placating someone or telling a white lie, you might do things to avoid diversity – and you might not know you are doing it.

An easy illustration of comfort zone is one we have witnessed countless times in our work. Our workshops usually take place over two or three days. There is never an arranged seating plan – and yet there is always a seating plan. On the first day, most participants choose to sit with (a) people they know or (b) people from their department. Without fail, when they arrive on the second day most take the same seat at the same table with the same people. You see children doing the same thing in a playground, teens doing the same thing at dances, even university students doing the same thing in new classes. It's all about your comfort zone. Now, take this same behavior and apply it in your own world – do you see comfort zones playing out in your workplace, your neighborhood, your community? Look at the Chinatowns, the Little Italys, the Little Havanas in North American cities – these are comfort zones. Such ethnic enclaves are not always "comfortable"; most evolve because of social and economic disparity. But comfort – like to like – is also a factor in their growth.

DARWIN, DIVERSITY & SURVIVAL

In the 19th century, English naturalist Charles Darwin put forward the idea that flexibility was a necessary survival skill. He used the term 'requisite variety' to describe the ability of organisms to adapt and evolve. This has great merit today. The world is too small to avoid bumping into diversity: religious, political, cultural, social or otherwise. If diversity is the enemy, we are in big trouble. Our world is becoming increasingly interconnected in new and sometimes frightening ways. The ability to adapt to change is necessary to our survival as a species.

> "It is not the strongest species that survive, nor the most intelligent, but the ones most responsive to change." - Charles Darwin

Corporate cloning is the antithesis of diversity. It means that people hire people like themselves, and it can refer to gender, race or physical ability, although there are laws to promote fair hiring practices and workplace diversity. It also happens on a more subtle level. If you are in charge of hiring a new recruit for your department, for example, chances are you will be drawn to a candidate whose appearance, dress, mannerisms and attitude are in tune with your own. You might also be drawn to those who share your ideas or interests. So while you may not hire someone who looks like you, you will probably hire someone who thinks like you: like will gravitate to like. There is nothing wrong with this, unless it is at the expense of the "unlike". But too much 'alike' leads to homogeneity. By avoiding diversity we are limiting our ability to benefit from diversity. A diverse workforce is a better workforce. The benefits are well-documented, from stronger employee morale to improved client relations to fewer interpersonal conflicts between employees. The wider variety of viewpoints and experiences of a diverse workforce also enhance creativity and productivity. Think about projects you have been involved with, whether at your job or as a volunteer in your community. Can you call to mind projects where you worked with people from similar socio-economic and religious backgrounds? How about projects where you worked with people from different backgrounds? How did diversity, or lack of it, impact your project? Were you able to make diversity your strength?

> *Ron: Diversity gets more real for me when I travel. When my wife and I fly to Singapore to visit her family, the shift to a culture halfway around the world is always mind-opening, but often in subtle ways. I can be reading the daily newspaper and something will jump out at me. The news media there is censored and managed by the government. Years ago, I remember reading a story on how great Singapore's education system was, and how the government was making sure everybody had a second if not a third language. That was front page news. Then, buried somewhere on page seven, there was a tiny update on the OJ Simpson trial – which was front page news on just about every American paper at the time. It made me ask myself, what is more news worthy, OJ Simpson's trial or the education of young people? It wasn't about being right or wrong, censored or uncensored; it was just interesting to see the world from a different perspective. That's the power of diversity.*

BLINDING OURSELVES TO DIVERSITY

Let's go back to the F card exercise. One of the reasons it is so disarming is that it takes the fear out of acknowledging that you may be missing something. You're not so sure about what you're sure of anymore. Maybe the other guy has a point, even if you don't agree – and maybe it's okay to disagree. Recognizing your blindness can help avoid lock-on/lock-out and put you on the road to acceptance of diversity. Politics provides a good example. One of the biggest political divides of recent years has been between supporters of President George W. Bush and his Republican policies and those of President Barack Obama and his Democratic policies. The Oliver Stone film, *W.*, provided a stage for this drama. We are not talking about the film critics here, but about our own circle of friends. Ron felt sympathy for President Bush as a man in over his head. His wife thought the film let Bush off easy. A close friend felt the film was a caricature rather than a three dimensional portrait. Gregg was surprised to find himself sympathetic to the man, but still questioned whether the film held him accountable. Such diversity of opinions from four people!

The multi-faceted response to the film underscores two important concepts. First is the value of the integral theory of partially right. If we take our various opinions, is it possible that our overall view of Bush can add up to a better, more informed opinion? Second is that blindness really is our problem. Perhaps it also takes a group of eyes to see all the different shades of grey that exist between black and white ... or your opinion and my opinion, your belief and my belief.

BE A DISPUTER

When we teach people how to unhook from limiting beliefs about themselves, we show them how to dispute and sanction the information and opinions being fed to them. We think this has tremendous implications for peaceful coexistence.

GIVING SANCTION[14]

When others describe you, it is up to you to either accept or reject their opinion. Acceptance is called giving sanction. You assimilate their opinion inside yourself. When it becomes part of your truth, you act in accordance with that truth.

The Pacific Institute teaches people to dispute the opinions fed into their mind. This is based on the research of Dr. Martin Seligman, a leading cognitive scientist and a long-time associate of The Pacific Institute. His research and landmark books on *Learned Helplessness* and *Learned Optimism* are central to TPI teaching on disputing negativity.

According to Seligman, your natural tendency might be more pessimistic or more optimistic, but it is your self-talk and your ability to dispute information that will ultimately determine your attitude. Negative people can become more positive by cultivating their disputing ability at the self-talk level. Instead of accepting everything you hear, learn to dispute the negatives and look for positives.

Diversity needs disputers. Rosa Parks, Nelson Mandela, Harvey Milk, Gandhi, Martin Luther King Jr. – the people who stand up for change are almost always disputers. The interesting counterpoint is that not every social change hero has been able to accept diversity. Disputing is not about denying all other realities or opinions. One-sided firebrands, while passionate and persuasive about their own beliefs, often rule out opposing opinions. They do not leave room for compassion or understanding.

Without acceptance of diversity, disputers can become bullies.

In today's media environment, we need to be especially vigilant about what kind of information we give sanction to and what gets assimilated into our opinions and beliefs. Media outlets have scotomas, too. Be a good editor when you read the paper or watch the news. Rather than tacitly giving sanction to what you're hearing, be a disputer. In a commencement speech at the University of Michigan in the spring of 2010, President Obama had similar advice for graduates heading out into the world.

> If we choose only to expose ourselves to opinions and viewpoints that are in line with our own, studies suggest that we become more polarized, more set in our ways. That will only reinforce and even deepen the political divides in this country. But if we choose to actively seek out information that challenges our assumptions and our beliefs, perhaps we can begin to understand where the people who disagree with us are coming from. ... It may make your blood boil; your mind may not be changed. But the practice of listening to opposing views is essential for effective citizenship."[15]

Question what you hear and how it impacts your worldview. Ask yourself whether the news, and your response to it, is out of proportion to the event. A random act of violence, for example, can be big news for several days. It is played over and over and over. You begin to think that random acts of violence are common. In fact, random acts of violence are pretty rare. And every day, there are millions of acts of coexistence going unreported. Media soundbites can feed our fears, threaten our sense of security and bolster our blindness. No wonder that some psychologists suggest over-consumption of news is not good for your mental health. Put yourself on a media diet.

DIALOGUE NOT DISCUSSION

Even before the invention of political correctness, there was tacit agreement that you did not talk about sex, politics or religion in social situations. We believe these are exactly the things we should be talking about. They are at the root of diversity avoidance. But we need to provide a framework in which to talk about them, and that framework is dialogue, not discussion. There is a difference. Researchers Glenna Gerard and Linda Ellinor describe dialogue this way, "In Dialogue we are interested in creating a fuller picture of reality rather than breaking it down into fragments or parts, as happens in discussion. In Dialogue we do not try to convince others of our points of view. There is no emphasis on winning, but rather on learning, collaboration and the synthesis of points of view."[16]

Dialogue	Discussion
To inquire to learn	To tell, sell, persuade
To unfold shared meaning	To gain agreement on one meaning
To integrate multiple perspectives	To evaluate and select the best
To uncover and examine assumptions	To justify/defend assumptions

SOFTEN THE EDGES OF YOUR TRUTH

World peace is our goal, coexistence is our path. Practicing diversity is a way to open our minds to the possibility of peace. It helps shine a light on areas where we may have locked-on and locked-out other opinions and beliefs. It promotes flexibility and adaptability in the face of change. It teaches us how to survive in a world where change is happening on a global level. It helps us soften our own sense of rightness and admit the possibility of partially right.

Darwin was right: if the human race is to survive, we need more than strength and intelligence – we need to be able to adapt to change. If you think back to our dialogue on how the mind works and how beliefs are formed, you begin to see that what you accept as truth is simply your interpretation of the truth, based on your past conditioning. Problems arise when our different interpretations of truth come into conflict, when our blindness prevents us from seeing the validity of another point of view. We reject this diversity. That is how religions can promote peace and goodwill, but still end up going to war. It is a stage of maturity to recognize that not everything we take in is the truth, the whole truth and nothing but the truth. It is a conditioned, or conditional, truth. This is why dialogue is so important. If we are to coexist, we need to facilitate dialogue among diverse truths. And we need to soften our edges when it comes to our own truths. We do not need to demonize or dehumanize others just because they do not share our truth.

We believe answers to some of the world's most critical challenges are rooted in our ability to recognize and accept diversity. So before you adjudicate another's truth, consider your own. What truths do you hold about your faith? What about your culture, your gender? When was the last time you thought about your skin color? What is the best advice you have taken from the opposite sex recently? Who is the most admirable person of a different color that you know? When was the last time you interacted with someone with a different truth? Taking the time to answer reflective questions will open your mind to the possibility that diversity is not something to fear but to embrace. In a world that every day grows smaller and more connected, diversity is our strength.

"If you grew up in a big city, spend some time with somebody who grew up in a rural town. If you find yourself only hanging around with people of your own race or ethnicity or religion, include people in your circle who have different backgrounds and life experiences. You'll learn what it's like to walk in somebody else's shoes, and in the process, you will help to make this democracy work."
- President Barack Obama, May 1, 2010, University of Michigan Spring Commencement

REFLECTIVE QUESTIONS

- Which of your best friends is most different from you? How are they different?

- What type of people are you afraid of? Why?

- Who do you idolize?

- Who do you demonize?

- When was last time you needed to apologize to someone different than you?

- What is the nicest thing you have done for a family member you do not like?

- When was the last time you looked for ways to coexist with someone of a different opinion or belief?

- Imagine a peace council charged with managing global coexistence. Who would be on your international dream team? How do they reflect diversity?

"Of course it is the same old story. Truth is usually the same old story."
Margaret Thatcher
Prime Minister of the United Kingdom, 1979 - 1990

PRINCIPLE 4:
NORMAL IS OUR ENEMY

If you thought "normal" was a good thing, think again. Your perception of normal plays a powerful role in your ability to peacefully coexist. We'll show you why. We'll also show you what you can do about it.

We all have a deeply-rooted sense of normal: I do, you do, they do. This perception of normal has a profound impact on our acceptance of diversity and our willingness to coexist. Principle 4 of *World Peace, Really!* is learning to recognize when normal is our enemy.

A WORLD GONE MAD

Ron: When I was a kid growing up in Tacoma, Washington, we used to have an air raid drill every Thursday at noon. It was like a fire drill, but when the sirens went off it meant a nuclear missile attack. Basically, we'd crawl under our desks, put our hands over our heads and kiss our butts goodbye. You got used to it; this is what we did every Thursday at noon. One day I was at home with my mom, two sisters and brother having lunch and the sirens went off. It was Wednesday. We panicked. My mom hurried us into the basement and we huddled into a corner under the stairs waiting for the bomb to go off. My mind was filled with images of people being melted. It turns out the siren was a planned drill – we had just missed the notice.

Welcome to the power of normal. In the 1950s, mutual assured destruction (MAD) emerged as a dominant military strategy between the world's two superpowers: the USSR and the USA. The basis of MAD was that if one side launched a nuclear attack of any size, the other side would immediately respond with full-scale use of its nuclear arsenal. Both attacker and defender would be destroyed: mutual assured destruction. The idea behind MAD was that neither side would launch a first strike because each knew the other would respond immediately on launch. There could be no winner. For almost 40 years, this insane form of coexistence was normal. Tensions between East and West are eased considerably, but these lessons do not just disappear. A whole generation is still coping with the lingering after-effects in their own personal sense of normal.

Ron: At my gym I found myself at a locker next to a couple of Russian guys. The first time I heard them talking a chill ran down my spine. It was a split second reaction, but it really surprised me. I laughed at myself. I mean, the Cold War has been over for 20 years! But my past conditioning had given me a cardboard cut-out image of Russians as bad guys. That conditioning was rooted in fear and that fear helped embed the bad Russian image as my normal. When I'm trying to coexist, you can bet normal is my enemy.

Even though the U.S. and Russia continue to work to reduce the nuclear weaponry we have pointing at each other, MAD is still in play. Still, we are moving away from the MADness. In 2009, the

United Nations Security Council unanimously endorsed a U.S.-drafted resolution calling for a nuclear weapons-free world. It was historic in that all 15 members of the UN Security Council voted in favor, including the five permanent members (China, France, Russia, United Kingdom and United States) who are normally opposed to any change in the status quo. In putting forward the resolution, President Obama acknowledged the skeptics, but said, "We must build new coalitions that bridge old divides... All nations have rights and responsibilities – that's the bargain that makes this work." The resolution must win the support of the public in individual nations and the debate over its value, even its sanity, is emotionally charged. It has ardent supporters and adamant detractors whose passion is underscored by their own individual sense of normal.

NORMAL FOR YOU

The question of what is normal is unanswerable because there is always a caveat. That caveat is that normal is defined in the context of you – what's normal for you. The power of normal might be universal, but there is no one-size-fits-all. Like everything else, it is much more complex. You have multiple concepts of normal. What is okay in a family or social setting might not be okay in a work setting. You do not deal with out-of-line behavior from your kids the same way you deal with it from employees. There are boundaries unique to each environment. Nothing throws those boundaries into such sharp relief as when someone steps outside them. You turn on the news one night and hear about a spouse killing a partner, a parent killing a child. The media interviews shocked friends and neighbors. "They seemed so normal," everyone says.

Normal social behavior is not only impacted by who you are, but also by where you live, what you look like, how you sound, how you dress, how much money you make and what you believe in. It all contributes to your normal of the moment. Subtle differences can have far-reaching impacts. Think about parents with different child-rearing philosophies or business partners with different ways of dealing with money issues. In *Love Leadership*, Gregg proposed an idea that had a lot of people in the corporate world scratching their heads: leading with love. Too often, when we are confronted with another normal, we default to defending our normal as the right way.

> *Gregg: After facilitating a workshop for staff at the ANNIKA Golf Academy™ in Florida I enjoyed a three-day skills improvement workshop with seven fellow golf enthusiasts. The first day our instructor, Charlotta Sorenstam, showed us a new grip. I really struggled with it. I was looking around, hoping I wasn't the only one having trouble and noticed something weird. Only two of us were actually trying to change our grip. Two were defaulting to their normal grip and not saying anything. The rest were giving the instructor all kinds of reasons NOT to change their grip. It was like listening to an inventory of "I can't". Did they really invest all this time and money just to stay the same? Or did their normal grip trump their investment in improvement? That's the power of normal.*

Normal is your comfort zone - a limited, well-defined psychological area where you can function effectively without experiencing uneasiness or fear. Step outside the boundaries and you feel uncomfortable, stressed. Your comfort zone can be so strong that you will go back to it, even when it is not really comfortable. We have all heard the stories of people being released from prison only to re-offend in order to get back to the one place they feel comfortable. Life outside is too hard, too confusing, too stressful. Normal is their enemy, because their normal is keeping them from living a full and free life.

The power of normal is exponential. The more you groove a normal, the deeper it gets and the more powerful it becomes. When you are young, every road you travel is new. With each new road you explore, you leave behind only light tracks. Go down the same road again, however, and the track gets deeper; go down many times and it becomes a rut. You don't even have to hold on to the steering wheel anymore, the rut holds you in place. When there is no rut, you have to pay attention and hold on to the steering wheel just to stay on track.

Your normal can be a rut that holds you in place. It has power over you. It defines what you believe, where you stand on issues, how you relate to others. Your normal not only has power over you, it controls you. It can make you believe that your normal is *the* normal and that anyone who does not share it must be abnormal. You need to figure out what is normal for you in order to understand where normal could be your enemy. By becoming aware of your normals, you see how they impact not only your behavior, but also your behavior toward other viewpoints. As with any kind of personal growth it requires self-examination. You need the insight in order to act to correct enemy normals. Start by learning how your normals form.

HOW DID I GET HERE?

You already know from Principle 1: Coexistence Is Our Goal, that you act in accordance with the truth as you believe and perceive it to be. You know that while your conscious mind is busy perceiving, associating, evaluating and deciding, your subconscious is sorting information into truths and your creative subconscious is acting accordingly – it is maintaining your sense of normal. If you break your normal down into its component parts you will find habits, attitudes, beliefs and expectations. We have seen the remarkable "ah-ha" people get when they understand the role habits, attitudes, beliefs and expectations play in their lives. Here's the basic theory.

We form habits as individuals, communities and countries. The beauty of habits is that they allow us to habitualize tasks. Watch a child learning how to brush teeth or a teenager learning how to drive; compare it to your own experience. Do you consciously remember brushing your teeth this morning? Do you even really remember driving to work? Your mind habitualizes a variety of tasks so that you can do more than one thing at a time. Some habits you knowingly create; others form without your conscious knowledge. Habits become an enemy when you habitualize things that do harm. Maybe when you get cut off in traffic it has become your habit to respond aggressively; maybe when you get depressed it has become your habit to drink or eat too much. There are habits that are helpful and habits that are harmful. You need to re-examine each to discover which are helping and which are harming you and your ability to coexist.

Attitudes add another layer. Over time, you form attitudes toward gender, ethnicity, nationality. Instead of categorizing these as good or bad, view them as an indication of how much you lean toward or away from someone or something. The US attitude toward Iraq is a lean away, for example, while the attitude toward Canada is a lean toward. Do you lean toward or away from Iraq? Do you lean toward or away from Muslims, Jews, Democrats, Liberals, universal health care, gay marriage, the death penalty? These leanings become automatic because your conscious mind has made its decision and your subconscious mind now accepts that decision as true. Your creative subconscious will ensure that you continue to act in accordance with this perceived truth, right or wrong.

HABITS + ATTITUDES + BELIEFS + EXPECTATIONS[17] = YOUR NORMAL

- Habit: a pattern of activity that has, through repetition, become automatic, fixed, easily and effortlessly carried out.

- Attitude: the direction in which you lean toward or away from something; a subconscious emotional response

- Belief: emotional acceptance of a proposition, statement or doctrine.

- Expectation: the prospect of a future embodiment of an abstract idea.

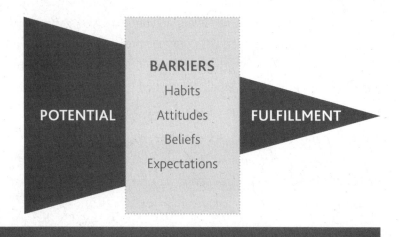

The biggest hitters in your perception of normal are your beliefs. You act in accordance with truth as you *believe* it to be. Remember, your beliefs are formed by how you think, and you think in three dimensions: words-pictures-emotions. If you are Jewish, for example, and you hear the word "Nazi", the word creates a picture which creates an emotion. If you are a Palestinian and you hear the word Israel, what picture does the word create, what emotion?

Words-pictures-emotions give power and conviction to our beliefs.

The final layer is expectations, either positive or negative. You have probably heard sayings like, "expect a bad day and get a bad day" or "be careful what you wish for (you just might get it)". Your creative subconscious plays a role in this. If a bad day is your belief, your creative subconscious will work to reinforce this belief. If you expect conflict with your neighbor, your creative subconscious will reinforce this expectation by coming up with opportunities for conflict: their yard is ill-kept, their dog barks too much, their garage light shines in your bedroom window. These are negative examples. You can also elevate your beliefs and expectations. If you expect to coexist peacefully with your neighbor, their yard may still need mowing, their dog may still bark and their garage light may still shine in your bedroom window, but now your creative subconscious is looking for opportunities to coexist. This shows you how important your beliefs and expectations are to coexistence. They are the foundations of your truth and you will act in accordance with your truth.

> Without an ongoing, conscious attempt to examine the truth of our normals, we just assume they are … normal.

WHERE NORMAL GETS ITS POWER

Normal draws its power from Gestalt. Gestalt theory says that human beings are always working to complete the incomplete. If you are normally punctual, order for you is being on time. When you are late, you drive over the speed limit to get where you are supposed to be on time. If normal for you is parting your hair on the left and you part it on the right, how long before your fingers itch to put it right? Normal draws its power from our ongoing search for order. Having your hair parted on the wrong side is not going to affect world peace, but the dissonance of having to work beside someone who looks, acts and talks differently than your sense of normal might affect your ability to coexist.

Cognitive dissonance maintains that you cannot hold conflicting ideas in your mind at the same time. When it happens, and it can be a frequent occurrence, you feel uncomfortable. This is dissonance. Dissonance is not a bad thing, because there is no growth without some tension. If you are getting input that conflicts with your current normal, that uncomfortable, itchy feeling is telling you to pay attention. You are holding conflicting beliefs and your mind is searching for a new normal. The risk is not that you will open your mind to new information, but that you will try to make the feeling go away by rushing back to your old normal.

> *Ron: Retiring from professional football was a strange and challenging time of my life. My normal had been competitive sports – locker rooms, an all-male environment and high-profile games every week. Normal life in the "real world" was very different. I needed new skills. Actually, my identity needed to change too. During the time that I was searching for a new identity, I didn't want to talk about football and being a football player. I didn't want the jock label, but I didn't know what else to talk about; neither did the people I met. It was an awkward time, like being a teenager again.*

What role does Gestalt play in world peace? Say you have grown up in a society where it is normal to be in conflict with your neighbors, such as in Northern Ireland in the 1970s, '80s and '90s. Communities were divided into Catholic and Protestant camps, and violence between the two was common. Now introduce a peace movement – what happens? People get very uncomfortable; they are thrown out of order. The conflict has become so embedded, so normalized, that it is uncomfortable for Protestant and Catholic alike to view themselves living in peace. This is the Gestalt of peace, and it takes courage and vision to work through it.

> **The world around you is always in Gestalt. You will feel dissonance as you change with it. It's perfectly normal.**

WHEN NORMALS COLLIDE

Our world is more connected than ever before. Diversity is delivered directly into our homes via television, internet and other media. Conflict results when that diversity causes our normals to collide. My normal says I am right and you, with your different normals, are wrong. Religion is one of the most powerful normals, so it is not surprising that it is also a major catalyst for conflict. The Abrahamic religions (Judaism, Christianity and Islam) share a common origin and a core belief in one God. This shared history forms the basis of diverse traditions and provides the foundation for each religion's interpretation of normal. Perhaps if we behaved according to the highest principles of our faith, we would not make war. We fight because our interpretation of faith is different. We become entrenched in our definition of normal, which makes everyone else abnormal. As you move along the spectrum of belief, the power of your normal increases. For example, a low-level believer might be comfortable questioning his or her own beliefs. A moderate believer might be open to the possibility that his/her normal is not everyone's normal and even a deeply committed believer can coexist with different beliefs. But for an extreme fundamentalist believer, the power of normal leaves no room for doubt, questions or other points of view.

Political belief is another powerful normal. When former President Bill Clinton travelled to North Korea to meet with leader Kim Jong-il, he did so in the hope of securing the release of two jailed American journalists. He accomplished this, but the visit sparked a highly charged debate in the United States. Many people were deeply upset. To them, the visit was a sign of weakness; it showed the U.S. placating a dictator, a member of the "axis of evil". Others praised the visit, saying there was no harm in talking. You can bet Mikhail Gorbachev met with a similar reaction in the U.S.S.R. when he began his program of economic and political reform. To some, he was a traitor; to others, a hero. Your viewpoint depends on the power of your normal.

IS IT NORMAL TO HAVE AN ENEMY?

It seems to be part of human DNA to have a villain. It goes back to fighting for peace – the action implies an enemy. And who's calling who the bad guy? For many, the people who carried out the September 11th terrorist attack are the bad guys. In Afghanistan, the people using smart missiles to kill Taliban insurgents but instead killing innocent women, children and elders are the bad guys. Our question is why not extend a hand for peace? Why stop at you're right and I'm wrong? Why not sit down and talk with the bad guys, at least then we have a chance of finding common ground.

DO WE NEED NORMALS?

We are not suggesting you dilute your beliefs. Strong beliefs guide us. As diverse human beings sharing a planet or as diverse family members sharing a house, we need common beliefs to help us adjudicate between right and wrong. Without it, we get dysfunction, anarchy. But if you lock on to your beliefs as the only truth, conflict is inevitable. A powerful belief in normal can be the enemy of coexistence.

Our global normal is evolving and the pace of evolution is accelerating. We are making progress in learning to play together, but we are also being held back by our old normals. Imagine being in a powerful speedboat and dragging a huge anchor behind you. You need an anchor, but there is a balance between an anchor that pulls you under and one that keeps you from drifting on the tide. The right anchor provides stability. Even then, you have to remember to lift it up before you move forward. If you try to pull the anchor along, it will slow you down – just like your normals. So yes, you need the power of normal to anchor you, but you also need the willingness to constantly evaluate your normals to ensure they are serving you well. Before you can meet someone outside yourself with coexistence, you have to face the internal enemy. By relaxing the grip of your beliefs, you are better able to appreciate that other people might have different beliefs. That is the balcony you need to be on to see that peaceful coexistence is possible.

One of the goals of this book is to challenge you to let your guard down a bit, take a hard look at your core beliefs, your normals. Are they working for you, are they working for the world? Are you strong enough to relax your view of normal to accommodate another view? Are you sure you are totally right, or is there room in your worldview for another partially right?

BING! YOU ARE NOW CROSSING A THRESHOLD

Normals sneak up on us. We behave or think a certain way and it gives us a reward – we feel cool, accepted, loved. So we do it again. We make a new normal. Wouldn't it be great if you knew when a behavior or attitude was going to solidify into a new normal?

It would be like having a GPS on your moral compass. Say you started to experiment with drugs. One day your GPS would go Bing! A gentle voice would say, "You are crossing a new threshold. If you continue on this path, you will not successfully reach your life goals." You know your behavior is a dead end street. The fact is, we do have those Bings!, but we do not always listen, or hear, or act.

> *Ron: At one time I did a lot of work in the aerospace community. I remember one facility in particular where they made intercontinental missiles – this was at the end of the 1980s. On the surface, the employees were very patriotic: they were in the business of defending their country. When we dug down deeper at the seminars, it began to be clear that there was some inner conflict. There was dissonance: on the one hand they were defending their country but on the other hand they were building killing machines. There's a price to pay in that kind of environment. It wears on your humanity, no matter how you justify it. I rationalized it, too. On surface level, I was sharing our education for all the right reasons, but at the end of the day, the company I was helping make more productive was building killing machines. Bing! I was in conflict with my deepest beliefs, now what do I do? I was helped by the U.S. and U.S.S.R. treaty on missile reduction, because that meant the government was ordering fewer missiles. It may have been bad for their business, but it was good news for me. It allowed me to facilitate their transition away from missile production into other areas. I wasn't entirely successful, but that Bing! did push me in other directions.*

We are constantly crossing thresholds. Unfortunately, we do not have GPS to monitor our actions, so we step across thresholds every day without realizing it. Hindsight is much clearer. You look back and see the turns you took in life and say, "Ah, *that* was a threshold. Shouldn't have done that or should have done this."

Your personal normal is constantly changing, which means your thresholds are dynamic, too. What was okay yesterday may not be okay today. When you were in grade school, what was normal in terms of how you treated the opposite sex? Apply this same normal in high school; still okay? Maybe not. How about university, your first job, your social circle? Our perception of normal changes as we mature, and so does our threshold for behaviors related to that normal. It might be forgivable for an eight-year-old boy to punch an eight-year old girl in the arm, but it is not okay for a 16 year-old, or a 27 year-old, or a 59 year-old.

Thresholds are created in workplaces, too. How many times in your working life have you ground your teeth together because someone said to you, "That's just the way we do things around here, don't ask me why." The "why" is that at some point a threshold was crossed and from then on the power of normal took over.

> *Gregg: I had been working a business association that had close ties to the provincial government in my home province. The association's management was discussing efficiencies and how to do things better. During the session it became clear that writing weekly updates to the government was taking a lot of time and energy that could be better spent doing other things. The managers were all wondering how to provide written reports in a more effective way when one of the "new guys" piped up and said why not just provide the update by phone, that's what he did. People around the table literally gasped. You didn't phone the minister, that's not how it was done. We talked about this and it became clear that the written reports did not evolve out of a governance procedure or rule, it was simply the way they had always done things. They had crossed a threshold without realizing it, and now it was a challenge to get them to think about creating a different normal.*

You may not have GPS to alert you that you are crossing a threshold into a new normal, but you do have your subconscious. The challenge is learning to listen to it. This is why learning how your mind works is so important: the more you know, the more perspective you gain on life. It is the vantage point of the higher balcony we talked about in the introduction.

CREATING A NEW NORMAL

Imagine your perception of normal like flying through life on auto pilot. You do not have to think about how you do routine things, you just do them. You fly on auto pilot every day: your morning routine, your route to work. The thing about auto pilot is that when you grab the stick to make a change, you only have control while you hold the stick; as soon as you let go the plane shifts back to auto pilot. Your normal does the same thing: you might change the way you think about an incident when you hear it on the news, but does it impact the way you think about the deeper issue? Have you made a change to the auto pilot program, or will you revert back to the same way of thinking, acting and believing as you did before?

There is an ebb and flow to our perception of normal. You may lean to the left at some point in your life, then maybe to the right. It is a continuum. Your normal is also situational. Every day, life hands you a new bunch of challenges, blessings and experiences. Where is your center of gravity today, what is your Kosmic address? The way you respond might depend on where you are on the continuum of normal. If you see a horrific crime on the news, you might feel justified in wanting to kill the person who perpetrated it – and maybe it is appropriate to feel that. But is it appropriate to act on it? Is it appropriate to make that your habit, attitude, expectation or belief?

You need normals - we all do. You also need to know what your normals are and how they can control you, because normal can be your enemy.

- Be aware of your normals. If you are aware of why you think the way you do, you have a much better chance of changing the way you think.
- Examine your normals. Dig down and examine the root cause.
- Approach the world with curiosity and interest.
- Recognize partially rights.
- Avoid labeling; labels are the first act of violence.

Understanding where your sense of normal draws its power will help you recognize thresholds – those moments when your inner GPS moral compass goes "Bing!, if I continue on this path I will not be successful in reaching my goals." This will help you make informed decisions about your behavior. It will also help you take advantage of the power of normal by making peaceful coexistence your new normal.

> We do not want our kids and grandkids to be normal – not our normal, anyway. We want them to be better. They are inheriting a world that is not our world. They need a new intelligence, a new sensibility. They need to learn from our generation, from our mistakes and our successes – and they do!

MEETING THE BEAR

Gregg: When I begin working with a client on corporate cultural transformation, I often begin with the bear story. The bear is hibernating at the beginning of the story. It sleeps through the cultural assessment process, which we do to measure how adaptable an organization is to change. The assessment is based on a numeric scale of one to 1,000: a high performing organization will score in the 700-800 range; a low performing organization will score in the 100-200-300 range. Organizations that fall in the 100-200-300 range are frequently those with a history of institutionalized behaviors and patterns. They are the clients who show the most dramatic improvements during the transformation process. Unfortunately, they are also the ones with the biggest bears. We'll get two or three years into a transformation, and the organization will be seeing positive changes in its culture at every level – and that's when the bear wakes up. The bear starts clawing back the momentum, resisting change, finding excuse after excuse to stop the process. The bear is the old normal. It is the same bear we face as we move toward peaceful coexistence. In moving toward peaceful coexistence, we can predict a backlash – the wakening bear. It will come out, whether from the depths of your own subconscious or from our collective subconscious, and it will growl and claw back momentum. It will resist change because it is fearful of change. This book is our anti-bear strategy.

In November 2008, American voters created a dramatic new normal when they elected Barack Obama as President. Up until that point, the normal was that a black president was impossible. Obama's election will go down in history as a milestone, like the end of slavery or universal suffrage. It led to a euphoric sense of possibility, but will the power of the old normal let the new normal develop? Many people would love this to be the new normal, but many want to return to their old normal. The collective evolution of a new normal is creating disharmony and dissonance; it is uncomfortable, awkward … and perfectly normal. The bear inside is waking up.

REFLECTIVE QUESTIONS

- What did you learn as a kid that you had to unlearn as an adult?

- Has it become normal for you to see certain people as one dimensional cardboard cut-outs?

- Is it normal to have an enemy? Do you need to have an enemy to make sense of the world? How – in what way? Why?

- Where is your normal held in place by fear? Do you want to change it? Why or why not?

- In what areas of your life would you like to create new normals?

- What beliefs remain non-negotiable for you?

- Can you remember the feeling of growing to a new normal, one that was your choice? Describe the positive sensation.

> *"When the power of love overcomes the love of power,*
> *the world will know peace."*
> Jimi Hendrix, American musician

PRINCIPLE 5:
LOVE IS OUR JOURNEY

You have explored how your mind works, identified your blind spots, uncovered your barriers to diversity and come to grips with the power of your normal. Now we're asking you to start applying the principles to building a more peaceful world. Your journey begins with love.

What does love have to do with coexistence? Everything. In order to have world peace, each of us needs to respect the dignity and humanity of our fellow human beings – that's our fundamental definition of love. But love for your fellow man (or woman) does not just happen, and life does not make it easy. So much can get in the way – the way we are raised and taught, our experiences at school, at home, in the workforce. Love is a journey, one we hope you begin in practice as well as in mind. Reading the book will only take you halfway; you need to bring yourself to the process. Answer the questions, reflect on your experiences, create your own peace goals. When you do, something special begins to happen. In the last three principles, we show you how to set goals that move you away from fear, hate and negativity, and toward love, adventure, optimism and peace. What better starting point than love? But how to get there?

NON-JUDGMENT, FORGIVENESS AND LOVE

The road toward love, and toward peace, has several gates. Pass through these and the journey becomes easier. The first is non-judgment: the ability to look at other people, other ideas, other viewpoints without judging them. You will not be able to love thy neighbor as thyself when you are judging what they wear, how they talk, what they belief. When you judge, you create scotomas. Your mind begins to look only at the things that validate your judgment and remains blind to those things that would prove your judgment wrong. To your creative subconscious, sanity is more important than truth. Practicing non-judgment throws open the door to other normals, other partially rights. It signals your subconscious that different viewpoints are not a threat to your sanity. When there is no rush to judgment, you have a better chance of seeing all sides to an issue, and that clears the way to move toward peace.

The second gate is forgiveness. In all of our lives, there are injuries and wrongs done to us by others. Deep cuts leave visible scars, but even small cuts can leave a lasting mark. Say you were bullied at school by a gang of toughs. Maybe they were streetwise kids who wore wild clothes and had dangerous habits; maybe they were well-dressed kids from well-off families; maybe they were kids of a different ethnicity. Now say you are interviewing job applicants and a young person comes in who reminds you of your childhood tormenter. You can bet that your past experience will play a role in how you deal with the applicant in front of you. There is a grudge buried in your mind, and that grudge is driving you away from forgiveness and back towards judgment. Your "grudgment" can impact your decisions in subtle ways: you might not hire people who subconsciously remind you of your bully, you may take an instant dislike to a neighbor or coworker, you might disregard the opinions of others without really listening to them. Your reaction might be more overt: you might do violence to others. And if we broaden our scale to nation level, you might go to war with other countries that bullied you. Non-judgment and forgiveness are necessary in order to increase your capacity to respect the dignity and humanity of others.

Judgment → Grudgment → No Love-ment

HATE IS ALSO A JOURNEY

Love is our journey, but it is also our choice. And it has a counterpoint: hate. If you stretch a diagonal line between love and hate, you will move through disdain, dislike, ambivalence, liking and caring. That is the journey. You choose the direction. As you increase your capacity to love, you move toward peace. You elevate your capacity for sustainable success by increasing your capacity for respecting the humanity and dignity of others.

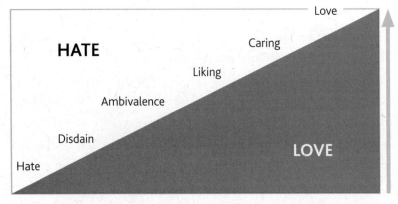

Gregg: A year or so ago, my daughters were staying at our condo in Mexico. Avery woke up one morning to find that money and several items had been stolen from her room during the night. The thought of thieves in my daughter's room while she was sleeping really got to me. My fear manifested itself as hate, and in my mind I acted on that hate by taking a baseball bat to the guy's legs. I say this with embarrassment, because I know better. In my book on Love leadership, I put forward a case for allowing love into leadership by saying love drives out fear. But fear for my daughter led me to judgment and then grudgment. The point is that I didn't stay there. It required a conscious effort to practice non-judgment. I told myself that they stole money and stuff, but they didn't harm to my sleeping daughter. I can't say I love them, but I can say I don't hate them. I no longer want to take a baseball bat to their legs. And that is the road to forgiveness and love ... and peace.

It is not always easy to "love thy neighbor". People like Hitler come to mind, the genocides in Yugoslavia or Rwanda, the treatment of North American Indians, of African Americans. Most of us can get to hate as quickly as we can get to love. In some situations, hate is easier than love. How do you apply love in a hate-inducing situation? You need to train yourself to take the high road. Try to curb your emotional involvement. Remain curious, open and rational. Avoid judgment. Bringing these qualities to a conflict situation can be highly effective in reducing the intensity of emotion and the degree of conflict. You might still have disturbances or frustrations, but now the people around you know that their personal dignity is not under attack. That's the first ground rule in leading with love: make it clear that whatever happens, you will not in any way diminish the dignity or humanity of the individuals involved in the dispute. If there is infringement on this ground rule, stop the discussion and go back to this rule. The world's greatest peace leaders understand the close relationship between hate and violent conflict and love and peaceful coexistence. Martin Luther King Jr.

summed it up when he said, "Let no man pull you low enough to hate him."

"Hatred paralyzes life; love releases it. Hatred confuses life; love harmonizes it. Hatred darkens life; love illuminates it."
- Martin Luther King Jr.

HOW FEAR GETS IN THE WAY OF LOVE

Fear and hate are closely intertwined. Hate begins with fear; fear enables hate. Fear of hunger and pain, fear of death, fear of something happening to our loved ones – all can spur us on to hateful actions. Trace hate deep enough and you will find fear: fear of losing identity, possessions, status, life. Fear is a tremendous barrier to love. If God is love, if love is the common denominator and we truly live in a universe of abundance, then reducing fear can contribute to coexistence. If we can get rid of fear and the deeply embedded habits, attitudes, beliefs and expectations that go with it, then we can get rid of hate.

> *Ron: A part of our brain does not make decisions, it simply reacts. In the blink of an eye, we get scared. Hate, it seems, comes on a little slower. If someone killed my family, like the innocent bystanders in a terrorist attack, I don't know what I would do. Part of me says I would burn this book. Then I would be gone, I would hit the road until my feet bled. I would have to be saved by God's grace; the spirit of the world would have to come to my rescue. But I'd like to think that I would not give hate a home; that I wouldn't let it consume me. I pray for that strength.*

Is it hatred that fuels ethnic cleansing? Are we killing people because we hate them or because we are fearful of them? Is it hatred that makes us refuse to listen to the opinions of world leaders such as Cuba's Fidel Castro, Libya's Muammar Gaddafi, Iran's Ahmadinejad or Venezuela's Hugo Chavez. Is it fear? Or is it legitimate anger? We will talk more about the role of legitimate anger a little later. For now, ask yourself what happens if we let people like Gaddafi talk. His maiden speech before the United Nations General Assembly in 2009 was a 96-minute rant that swung from the bizarre to the insulting to the mundane. But even the political analysts agreed that amid all the hyperbole there were several valid points. Few people have listened to the full speech, but how many have listened to any of it? Most of us are content to get our news in short soundbites. In doing so, we tacitly agree to the bias of the news media who are deciding which soundbite to play. Who decides what part of that 96-minute speech you should hear? This kind of media communication leads to over simplified and often one-sided presentation of key issues. We believe it is one of the reasons most of us form cardboard cut-out images of different cultures and ideas.

> "I think, therefore I fear."
> - David Burns, *When Panic Attacks*

We do not need to be so afraid of each other. An airing of opinions is healthier than going to war over them. Having said that, a healthy airing of opinions might not prevent a war; armed response might still be necessary to stop a genocide such as Kosovo. But if the global community is more open to listening to different points of view, and if different opinions put out there for everyone to see and discuss, could we forestall some of the issues that lead to war? Yet we are increasingly afraid to do this. Instead, we get upset when differing points of view are aired or when "bad guys" get to air their views on television. They are spreading hate, we say. That might be true, but do you contain hate by gagging other opinions? Does that really work? What happens if we let that person's rant stand on its own merit? What if we counter hate and fear with openness, curiosity, non-judgment and rationality. What if we continue to respect that person's dignity and humanity? That is the choice. Are we brave enough to do it?

Hate is the external face of our fear; fear is what is happening enough inside us. Fear can enable hate and disable love. To get to coexistence, we need to address our fears with love … and we need to start the journey within ourselves.

WHY FEAR IS A BARRIER

"Love thy neighbor as thyself" is a version of the Golden Rule shared by many world religions. It sounds simple enough … except you're scared to death. Loving your neighbor is a surrender you are not willing to make because you have been hurt by those you love. The people you trusted to love you unconditionally hurt you. You cannot love your neighbor because you do not trust your neighbor. Perhaps the problem goes even deeper; maybe you do love your neighbor as yourself – that's the problem. You are looking in a mirror and you do not like what you see.

We begin our lives, or at least we hope we do, with the love of our parents. Too often, though, this is where love and life first start to go wrong. Maybe we are traumatized by bad parenting practices or exposed to poor role models. As children, we learn that there are things that go bump in the night, things to be afraid of. The real sin comes later, when as adults we do not question what we grew up with. Was the way we were raised or disciplined conducive to loving our neighbor, or is this where the seeds of hatred and fear were planted? It is a question we need to ask ourselves, otherwise we normalize our fears, give them power and pass them on to our own children.

> *Gregg: The most memorable taxi ride of my life was a short trip from my hotel in Seattle to the airport. The driver was an 85-year-old Jewish American man who had survived Hitler and the Holocaust. He immigrated to the United States and talked openly about how much he loved America. But when he talked about Hitler, it was like he was living those terrible years all over again. His voice was full of passion, anger and hate. He has carried that fear and hate all his life. I make no judgment, because I cannot even imagine what he survived. For me, it was a profound lesson on love and hate, and the toll they take on our lives.*

'HERE THERE BE DRAGONS'

Before the concept of a spherical earth took hold, if you sailed too far west you knew, beyond a doubt, that the world would come to an abrupt end and you would plunge into the abyss. Maps signified unexplored portions of the world with phrases like, "here there be dragons". As far as mapmakers were concerned, there very well could be. How scary is that? That was then and this is now, you say; humanity has evolved beyond such fears. We have, and yet we haven't. Off the top of your head, how many doomsday scenarios can you name? The latest is that a cataclysm will cause the end of the world as we know it in 2012. It is based on an interpretation of the ancient Mayan calendar. The idea is rejected by scientists and Mayan scholars, but Amazon.com nonetheless lists over 150 books (and counting) on the 2012 doomsday scenario.

This is just one of many examples of how we are encouraged to be afraid. What is at work here? We believe many of the old tried and true ways of handling diversity are no longer up to the task

– the complexity of the world today far outstrips that of 1910 or 1810 or 1510. Confronted by a mass of information and ideas, we become fearful. This is one of the themes echoed in *High Noon: 20 Global Problems, 20 Years to Solve Them*[18]. In discussing the challenges facing our world, the author J.F. Rischard identifies two commonalities: the problems are getting worse and our normal responses are not working.

Every generation has its high noon. High noon is defined as both a time of confrontation or conflict and a time of creative transformation. The world has gone through many high noons. Every time we think, "something's gotta give", something does. The human race finds a way to adapt and survive. One reason is that the human brain continues to evolve, and the evolution isn't over yet. It is a point in our favor, but keep in mind that the human race has only just arrived at this level of consciousness. If you time travelled back 500 years to the days of Henry VIII, you would find humanity at a very different level.

Do you believe the world is more peaceful today than it was yesterday, or less peaceful? If your only source of information is the nightly news, daily paper or online webcast, your answer might be 'less peaceful'. But there are other sources that say we are living in a greater state of peace than ever before. For example, do an internet search on "Human Security Report". The 2009 report indicates that armed conflicts, war death tolls, military coups, refugee numbers, international crises and genocides have all declined since the end of the Cold War. A 2006 brief stated, "Notwithstanding the escalating violence in Iraq and the widening war in Darfur, the new data indicate that from the beginning of 2002 to the end of 2005, the number of armed conflicts being waged around the world shrank 15% from 66 to 56."[19] Is this viewing the world through rose-tinted glasses? Well, the report also notes that terrorist incidents and campaigns of organized violence against civilians have both increased in the same period. Even knowing this, it is our strong belief that the world is moving toward greater peace. But we also believe there are very real, very big challenges ahead.

As human knowledge has expanded, our consciousness has evolved. We are at a point where we are able to consider new perspectives and handle new challenges in a peaceful way. But when you add cultural, economic and geo-political tension, it creates a set of conditions that favor conflict. In order to have coexistence, we must find a way to turn our high noon into a creative transformation rather than conflict. It is uncharted territory. Our goal of this book is to get you thinking about peace in a practical way. This principle, Love is Our Journey, is essential. Love is a choice that impels you to respect the dignity and humanity of fellow human beings, that impels you to turn away from negativity and choose optimism, something we talk about in the next chapter. It is a both choice and a life-long journey.

> Is the world more or less peaceful, more or less deadly? Challenge your assumptions and expand your viewpoint at www.humansecurityreport.info or www.TED.com (search 'world peace')

THE WAR STARTS INSIDE

Conflict originates in Gestalt. You feel conflicted because you cannot reconcile what you are seeing, hearing, touching, smelling or tasting with your inner "truth". Given the chance, your brain will come to the rescue and restore order by reconciling the new knowledge. In fact, the conflict actually creates the ability to reconcile. This is a process called synthesis. Understanding how your brain responds to conflict is important. It provides insights you can use to work through it. Otherwise, when faced with conflict your knee jerk response is to seek relief, and you do that by taking your internal conflict and externalizing it – you start a war. It might be a war of words with a colleague or a spouse, but it could also be a bigger war with your community or your neighbors.

> *Ron: When you have love and respect, you still have conflict – but it's different. When it comes to resolving conflicts, I don't have to look any further than my relationship with my wife. For Calli and I, arguing is like being caught in a tropical downpour. We both get soaked. Love is knowing that the sun is shining somewhere behind the storm clouds. We'll dry out and warm up in an hour, or tomorrow at the latest.*

Conflict is not good or bad; it is your reaction that gives it its flavor. You can groove a habit of responding badly to conflict. The conflict itself could lead to confrontation and violence, but it could also stimulate creativity and be a catalyst for problem-solving. It could also be a pathway to love. The story of Jesus turning the other cheek is a classic example of responding to conflict with love. But to follow this path, we need to get beyond the dragon – our fear.

Conflict is not inherently good or bad; it might even be necessary. The good or bad happens in your response to dealing with conflict.

WHAT IS YOUR CAPACITY FOR FORGIVENESS?

Gregg: My daughter was reading a book called The Sunflower by Simon Wiesenthal for a university philosophy class. It is based on Wiesenthal's experience in a Nazi concentration camp during World War II. He was taken to see a dying Nazi soldier, who wanted to ask for forgiveness from a Jew. Years later, Wiesenthal asked leading intellectuals what they would have done in his shoes He collected their responses in the book. The question is timeless. What would you do? What are the limits of your forgiveness? If you have a clear philosophy to guide you, you have an answer. Without religious, social or political normals, how do you make such a decision?

How do you love someone who hates you? How do you love someone who kills your family? What about people who fly passenger planes into buildings and kill thousands? When some harm has been done to you or your family, you might not get to forgiveness but you need, for your own peace of mind, to at least get to reconciliation. It is not quite peace and not quite love, but it is a step in the right direction. And if you can get to forgiveness, you not only release the one who did you harm, you release yourself.

Our basic premise is peaceful coexistence. Flying a plane into a building is not coexistence; using violence to terrorize a population into submission is not coexistence. There are people who dehumanize and people who do violence. But there are more people choosing not to do violence, not to demonize, not to label. If we cannot solve the riddle of those who would do violence, then perhaps we can focus on the many who do good. History is full of them, from the Ten Commandments of Moses, to the U.S. Bill of Rights, to the UN Charter of Rights.

> "People learn to hate, and if they can learn to hate, they can be taught to love."
> - Nelson Mandela

PAYING ATTENTION

Ron: I was in the barbershop the other day. It was crowded with fathers and their sons. Next to me, two four-year-olds started fighting over a video game. One boy got the game, the other walked away crying. I am haunted by the smug look on the face of the boy who "won". He learned something that day and I don't think it was something good. Sure, he learned how to win, but he didn't learn how to coexist. He didn't learn that there was another choice. Maybe I should have intervened and facilitated coexistence, but I felt stuck. Wasn't that the father's job? He wasn't paying attention and I didn't know what to do. I still don't. But failure is a learning experience. I don't kick myself, I pay attention so that I can respond better in the future. Now here's a seed planted in my brain – next time I will do better.

If your life lessons are all about winning and beating the other guy, are you learning about coexistence or are you learning about power? When you are witness to a conflict, what do you do?

EXPAND THE GAP BETWEEN STIMULUS AND RESPONSE

Conflict resolution has been studied and discussed for ages. Books have been written about it. In *The 8th Habit*, Stephen Covey[20] writes that "Between stimulus and response there is a space. In that space lies our freedom and power to choose our response. In those choices lie our growth and our happiness."

Being able to create a gap between stimulus and response is not something that comes naturally to most people. Our limbic system has a built-in fight or flight response, though cognitive science is now suggesting it is actually a fight, flight or freeze response. Using the lessons in this book can help cultivate greater mindfulness about your own intuitive responses – you can use that new mindfulness to help you build the space, and the freedom of choice that comes with it. But if you want something more definitive, try out the U.S. Navy's principles of conflict resolution.

U.S. NAVY PRINCIPLES OF CONFLICT RESOLUTION[21]

- Think before reacting
- Listen actively
- Assure a fair process
- Attack the problem, not the person
- Accept responsibility [avoid blaming others]
- Use direct communication [speak your point of view without loaded words]
- Look for interests [find out what is truly at issue]
- Focus on the future
- [Look for] options for mutual gain

LOVE BEGINS WITH HEALING

Conflict will happen, always. How we respond to conflict will determine our future, on a personal level and a global level. Love is a way to mitigate a knee-jerk, violent response to conflict. But love requires reconciliation. To reconcile means to cause to coexist in harmony, but it is also about recognizing compatibility. It takes courage, because there is a lot of fear. It is also hard. It requires a conscious act of will to get our minds to look for blind spots, to welcome diversity, to move beyond our power of normal.

Love and peace are the ultimate goals, but there is a middle path that can take us there – coexistence. Coexistence does not mean I agree or disagree with you, we simply agree to peacefully coexist. It happens in the best of families. Growing up, you may have issues with your parents or your siblings. You might not agree with each other's choices in life, and you may not resolve those differences, but chances are you will still find a way to coexist.

> *Ron: At the end of our lives, all the philosophizing and all the arguments become simple in the face of love and death. My brother is a cool guy. We are a number of years apart in age, so we've only gotten to know each other as adults. We are sitting together now. Yesterday, when I came to visit, he got out of bed and came half way across the room to greet me. Pretty amazing for a guy dying of cancer. But he is the strong one right now. When I look at his face, I can see everything he believes in. I can see God in his eyes. It is miraculous but completely natural. All the pretence is gone, all the tomorrows are gone. It's just him, like a newborn baby. He is at peace.*

THE GOAL COMES FIRST

So how do you begin the journey toward peace? How do you live the principle of love? Start with the premise we introduced in principle 1, **You act in accordance with the truth as you belief it to be**. This phrase is at the heart of any personal transformation you wish to make in your life, and it is at the heart of our belief that world peace really is possible. In order to coexist with other opinions, beliefs and faiths, you need to make it a goal. Yes, we're really asking you to set world peace as your goal.

> The goal comes first, then you perceive. You don't need to know HOW. You need to know WHAT and WHY.

MAKE IT REAL

You, as a human being, are goal-oriented. It is in your nature, possibly in your DNA. To reach your goal, you must have a clear picture in your mind. In our TPI workshops we teach this as I x V = R[22]. Imagine your goal with such Vividness that it becomes a Reality stored in your subconscious. Another way to describe this is words-pictures-emotions. In your mind, words trigger pictures which trigger emotions. If someone calmly swears at you in Swahili, you probably will not react. You have the words but not the picture or the emotion. If the strange words come with an angry face and a raised voice, you have a picture and an emotion.

In setting a peace goal, let's say you have a neighbor you cannot seem to get along with. What happens if you make your goal, love this neighbor as myself? Can you build the word-picture-emotion? Can you create I x V = R? If not, imagine that neighbor as a fellow human being. Your goal is simply to respect the dignity and humanity of that person. Attach pictures and emotions to the words, what does this look and feel like? Now, can you see your goal? This is what we mean by love is our journey; it happens one step at a time.

MOVE TOWARD YOUR GOAL

Your creative subconscious is goal-oriented[23]. One of its job functions is to move you toward you what you are thinking about, which is why goals are so important. Your creative subconscious will move you toward a goal that is well imagined, vivid and real. This is also a journey. Your creative subconscious might overshoot the goal, veer off course or get sidetracked. This causes negative feedback – an itchy, "things don't feel right" feeling. It's okay. This is Gestalt at work.

The goal in your mind and the reality of your situation don't match; you have dissonance. Don't avoid or shut down the negative feedback; listen to it. Your creative subconscious is trying to tell you that you need a course correction. There are no mistakes, just opportunities to correct your course to achieve your goal. Dissonance can also inspire creativity. When your outside doesn't match your inside, it clicks into overdrive to find solutions. As far as your creative subconscious knows, your sanity is at stake.

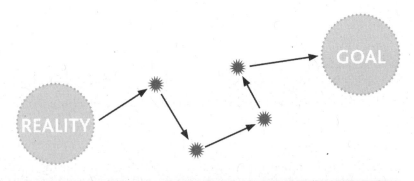

IGNORE THE "HOW", FOR NOW

Watching the nightly news, you might wonder how world peace is possible when we cannot even get along in our own communities? Start by forgetting the "how". Right now, what you want is more important than how you achieve it. Your mind will move toward what you are thinking about, so the first step toward world peace is making peace your goal. Focus on what you want. **"What" comes first, "how" comes later**[24]. Focus on building your goal into a clear, vivid image. What does peaceful coexistence look like? What does it feel like? Build the "what". Maybe your wish for world peace is rooted in a deep desire for peace in your marriage. What does that feel like? Maybe you want a more optimistic culture in your workplace or more harmony in your community.

If you can embrace this high-sounding principle of love as our journey, you can be the miracle in your own life. There is tragedy in the world; there is violence; there are people who have suffered unbelievable traumas. Despite the trauma and tragedy, we believe world peace is possible. We may not have all the answers, and the principles we offer are concepts you may have seen or heard before. What we want you to take away from this chapter is another viewpoint, one based our experience using a cognitive approach to helping people get their lives back. We have seen peace and peaceful coexistence happen where no one thought it was possible. It is possible, but peace is not about fixing everyone around you; the change starts inside. Love is a journey … and an adventure. Read on.

REFLECTIVE QUESTIONS

- Do you ever casually use the word "hate" to describe how you are feeling? How is that not accurate?

- What have you learned through fear, especially about yourself or other people?

- Who do you hate? Why?

- Who do you distain? Who do you like or dislike? Why?

- Who do you care about? Who do you love? Why?

- What makes you despair?

- What gives you faith in the human race?

- Who do you share your fears with?

- Do you believe you live in a loving environment? If not, what could you do to change it?

- Think of a time when you forgave someone? How did it feel?

- Have you ever asked someone for forgiveness? How did it feel?

> *"The real voyage of discovery consists not in seeking new landscapes, but in having new eyes."*
> Marcel Proust – French novelist and critic

PRINCIPLE 6: ADVENTURE IS OUR FRIEND

World peace is an awfully big adventure, so big it is tempting to shrink from it. That's a mistake. Too often, you set goals based on what you believe you can achieve right now, with the resources you already have. We believe in setting goals based on what you really want. Make it so vivid you can taste it. Do not worry about how, focus on what. That's the adventure.

At this stage of the book, you have a better idea of how your mind works, how your beliefs are formed and how those beliefs control not only how you act but how you think. You are more aware of your blind spots, more willing to step out of your comfort zone and to dispute the "truths" fed to you. You may or may not be convinced that your worldview is only partially right, but if you are still reading at least you are keeping an open mind. You are beginning to see with fresh eyes. All of this says something about your belief in world peace.

You have also learned how to make peace your goal, to put action behind the principles laid down in previous chapters. Now the adventure really begins. We are not going to pretend the road to peace isn't bumpy. It is, but the bumps are part of the adventure. To embrace peace means being willing to embrace *all* the elements of the journey; not just the love, harmony and acceptance, but also the anger, fear and conflict. That is what Principle 6 of *World Peace, Really!* is about. On this road trip, adventure is your best friend.

....

The goal in your mind will not match the world around you; that creates dissonance, which opens the door for your creative subconscious to generate ideas for achieving your goal.

....

Ron: This idea of coexistence has been part of my life for quite a while. Not surprisingly, my peace consciousness was born in the 1960's, like a lot of people. It is so deeply embedded in me that I couldn't shake it even if I wanted to. At first it felt like I was just looking for affirmation that peace was possible. Then it became a career in applied psychology. But that afternoon in the 7-Eleven® brought peace and coexistence into focus for me in a new way. The opportunity was right there in front of me, probably always has been. It happened again in the barbershop, and, when I think about it, has happened many times before and since. The moral of the story is that invitations to be an active part of "world peace" present themselves every day. Small opportunities and, just maybe, big ones. Some part of the adventure is always within your reach. How cool is that?

THROW YOURSELF OUT OF ORDER

By setting goals based on what you really want, without trying to figure out how you are going to achieve them, you will throw yourself out of order[25]. Learning how to throw yourself out of order is a great tool. It uses the power of cognitive dissonance to help you move toward a goal. We talked about this in Principle 4: Normal is Our Enemy; that you cannot hold conflicting concepts in your mind at the same time. Your mind wants order and such conflict is disorder. To restore order, your mind will move toward the dominant image. This means your goal must be stronger than any doubts you may have.

But how do you strengthen your goal of peace? Throw yourself out of order – do something different. Start by adding more diversity to your life. Make a friend out of someone who is not like you. Call and ask to visit a Sikh temple, a mosque, a synagogue, a church. Explore the ethnic restaurants in your community and ask your waiter what they recommend. Change the way you get your news: read two separate news stories on the same issue. Instead of watching headline-style news, watch an in-depth interview with a world leader. Better yet, watch an interview with a world leader you don't like. Visit www.TED.com and watch talks with titles that challenge your comfort zone. If you feel stressed, remember that it is eustress – the good kind. The goal of Principle 6 is not to be comfortable, but to be adventurous.

A friend, Dr. Soosan Latham, demonstrated this in a unique way while teaching a class on immigration. At the beginning of the class, she asked her students to identify the country or culture they liked the least – then she made that country/culture their project. They were asked to learn about the culture they disliked and to make a presentation on that culture following appropriate social norms. The student presenting on Iran split the class into male and female sections, required all the women to cover their heads, then turned and presented to the men without acknowledging the women. The dialogue that followed was an exploration, first, of how this made people feel and, second, of the cultural dictates and traditions behind it. It was not about deciding right and wrong; it was about exploring the possibility of coexistence between very dissimilar viewpoints. Optimism requires a mind open to new learning.

> *Ron: My wife's cousin Victor trades commodities for Shell Oil in Asia. Recently, he was visiting us and I caught him watching Fox News. I stay away from loud, opinionated pundits, so I said, "Victor, what are you doing? Fox News is so biased!" He responded, "It's important for me to take in all opinions. I need to know what everybody is thinking. That's part of my job." I thought, "Touché, Victor." There's a heck of a lesson there: sometimes the adventure is just listening to the other guy's point of view.*

Repeat after me ...
I am comfortable being uncomfortable.
I am comfortable being uncomfortable.
I am comfortable being uncomfortable. I am...

ALERT YOUR MIND TO THE POSSIBILITY

Just declaring that you want world peace will not make it happen. Establishing peace as your goal, however, will open your mind to the possibility of peace. **The goal comes first, then you perceive;** you perceive because you now have the necessary catalyst to bring your reticular activating system online.

My what? Your reticular activating system, or RAS, is a remarkable mental filter. It analyzes the stream of information that your senses (sight, sound, touch, taste and smell) are constantly feeding into your brain, then it screens the relevant from the irrelevant. As your eyes are scanning the words on this page, your ears might be picking up the sound of someone walking past your office, the hum of your computer, a cat meowing in the alley. Your taste buds are telling you the coffee is a bit too strong while the goose bumps on your skin are telling you the room is a bit too cool. This is just a fraction of the sensory input you are receiving. If you are concentrating on this book (and we hope you are), your reticular activating system has either pushed this input all into the background or tuned it out completely. Your RAS also scans for threats. You might ignore the sound of branches against your window, but the sound of footsteps on your back steps will prick up your ears.

Your RAS zeroes in on input your mind has tagged relevant or important. Set a goal and your RAS will reprogram itself to search out the opportunities. Set coexistence as a goal and you open your mind to the possibilities because your RAS is now actively scanning for those opportunities. What you deem relevant or important is constantly changing. When you go shopping for a new car, for example, you see car ads everywhere: in the newspaper, on bulletin boards at work, on signs posted in car windows.

When you set a new goal, you change the settings on your reticular activating system. Now it is scanning for information relevant to your new goal. Learn to use your RAS and your life becomes a great adventure. You set bigger, bolder goals and your RAS identifies bigger, bolder possibilities. Will you be able to end the war in Afghanistan or gang violence in big cities, maybe not; but you will see more opportunities to promote peace and coexistence in your own life.

RETICULAR ACTIVATING SYSTEM[26]

Of all the concepts we offer in this book, we believe the reticular activating system (RAS) is one of the most helpful ... and hopeful. Your RAS is a network of neurons in the brainstem that is involved in consciousness, regulation of breathing and transmission of sensory stimuli to higher brain centers. It screens the information bombarding your senses and filters out repetitive or non-essential stimuli. It only lets through information of value to you, everything else gets locked out. When you set a new goal, you change the settings on your reticular activating system. Now it is scanning for information relevant to your new goal. This includes information of value to your goal as well as information that could threaten your goal.

AFFIRM THE GOAL

In any dialogue on world peace, there is always a "but". "Yeah, I'd like to believe peace was possible, but—." "We could accept that way of thinking, but—." Ask yourself whether your reticular activating system is looking for the "but" or the opportunity? If you are coming up with a lot of "buts" maybe you need to examine your goal: is it coexistence or is it coexistence on your terms? "I'm right, you're wrong" is one of the bumps on the road we need to get over. Like any new idea, the goal of peace or coexistence is one you must affirm, over and over, in order to change your belief. Every day, affirm that peace is your goal and that you are coexistence in action. Your RAS will screen for opportunities and threats; it is up to you to act.

BUMP! CONFLICT IS UNAVOIDABLE

With so much diversity in the world, different ideas and beliefs are constantly bumping against each other. Conflict is unavoidable, yet many of us try. We go out of our way to avoid certain parts of town, certain people, certain discussions. When world peace is your goal, conflict becomes part of the adventure. Before you decided to embark on this adventure, you might have left the room if people started to argue or you might have picked a side and jumped into the fray. Now, coexistence is pushing you in different ways. You still might want to pick a side, but coexistence whispers in your ear that there are two sides to every argument. You might want to leave the room, but with your goal in mind and your RAS on high alert, coexistence is opening your mind to the possibility of a resolution.

> *Gregg: I've always seen myself as conflict avoidant, but you can't spend 25 years as a seminar leader without running into conflict. I've had to learn to deal with it head-on. Sometimes the conflict is outside me. I've had to jump in and mediate heated arguments in workshops. I push my chair between the combatants to stop the volleys back and forth, then I sit down and say let's talk. Once they're talking, I can back my chair out of the way and let coexistence re-establish itself. It's harder when the conflict is aimed at me. There is always push-back when you're introducing new ideas, but I've facilitated sessions where someone has made the push-back personal. I grab my chair again, sit down and say let's talk. Face to face, I generally discover the person wants a resolution to whatever is bothering them, and that opens the door to coexistence. Lately, I've come to realize that I am no longer conflict avoidant. In fact, I actually look forward to conflict because it opens the door to a resolution.*

....

Bumps along the way are part of the adventure. Don't be afraid.

....

> *Ron: I've been doing this work for almost 30 years and it still has the power to move me. Not long ago, I was facilitating TPI's* Discovering the Power in Me™ *education for people*

dealing with sudden disability. One of the participants was Cyril, a 72-year-old Vietnam vet. I could tell there was something going on with him, and on the morning of the second day he stood up and said, "Yesterday was the most important day of my life. I had declared myself dead. I'm diabetic, I've had a kidney transplant and I need another one. But I came in here yesterday and I learned about self-talk. I couldn't believe I was my own worst enemy. I have a lot of life left." It was an amazing moment, but it wasn't the end of the story. Cyril decided to walk home that day. It was a 3.5 mile trek and there were a bunch of hills he didn't remember, so pretty soon he says he was goal setting from telephone pole to telephone pole. Two blocks from home it starts to rain and he gets drenched. When he gets in the door, his wife goes ballistic. "Don't you know you're sick!" Her anger was rooted in her fear for him. That's the adventure: you might have the most important day of your life, then you bump into someone else's reality and there's conflict, even anger.

BARK! ANGER IS MANAGEABLE

Gregg: I have three kids so I've mediated my fair share of arguments over the years. I remember one situation where I was trying to make peace between my son and middle daughter. It turns out that Avery barked at Brogen because Katelyn barked at her because I barked at Katelyn because I was upset with Sandra. It wasn't until we unpacked the day at dinner that night that we realized Sandra had brought her anger home because of an incident with a woman at the grocery store. The conflict arose outside our home but ended up squarely within it. The anger came home with the groceries.

Much of the time, fear is fueling our anger. Anger is a legitimate reaction to fear. You might be afraid of losing something or someone. You might see the situation as an incursion on your personal boundaries. Managing your anger is essential to coexistence. Unmanaged, anger can morph into grudges, IOUs and all kinds of toxins that do not serve you well. But how do you coexist with someone who is angry with you? Can you remain level-headed when someone is yelling at you or do you yell back? If your goal is coexistence, you will find yourself more and more able to stand in the face of anger and not get angry yourself. Instead of labeling or making the other person wrong, you are now able to see that they may be partially right. You can see past the anger and recognize that some of what they are trying to impart is information, a point of view, a feeling, even their own fear. These insights help you manage your response.

> *Ron: I'm standing on the street one day saving a parking space for a disabled client. He calls me on his cell for directions, realizes he's overshot the spot and has to turn around. He uses a driveway down the road to make a U-turn. This brings the owner out in a hurry and he's furious. He starts ripping at my client so I head down to straighten him out. Well, he turns his anger on me. He's yelling and his face is inches from mine. He said, "You people are always turning cars in my driveway and sometimes my little granddaughter is out here playing." Fear for his grandchild's safety was behind his anger. I went from rising anger to a kind of peace. He wasn't any less angry, but I let him vent; I let him be right. In that instance, I was strong enough to manage my own anger and coexist.*

BING! COMPETITION CAN BE GOOD OR BAD

> *Ron: I played in the National Football League (NFL) for five years and I wouldn't have been as successful if I wasn't competitive. On the field, the competition is one-on-one. You inevitably get humbled. When you're a professional athlete, the reality is that there's always going to be someone bigger and better coming up behind you, and you learn there is a limit to your physical talent. In a way, it was a blessing to bump my head on the ceiling of my ability to compete. By my late 20s, I got most of that kind of competition out of my system. I had to look for other ways to grow.*

One of the ways we build self-worth in our society is by competing against others and winning. We compete in sports, in school, at work and socially. If we compete and fail, we feel devalued; if we compete and win, our self-worth soars. Competition certainly has its place, but we need to agree on what constitutes healthy competition. In terms of world peace, unhealthy competition is about physical domination – you see it in everything from school yard bullies to large scale wars. But domination means other things too. You might want more money than the other guy, or a bigger house, a cooler lifestyle, better toys, smarter kids ... whatever. The underlying theme is that you have more, they have less. You win, they lose. The flip side is when they win, you lose. They are bigger, better, smarter, stronger. Whichever side you land on, competing to dominate is a barrier to coexistence.

On a global scale, competition that dominates leads to strife, violence, war. Every age has experienced the ravages of war, but we live in a different age – the age of MAD. Despite the end of the Cold War, there are still enough missiles pointing around the globe to create a nuclear holocaust. There can be no winner in a nuclear war or a nuclear missile in the wrong hands; the whole planet loses. If that is not a definition for unhealthy competition, we don't know what is. In 2008, the drive to compete in no-holds-barred capitalism just about triggered an economic MAD. The thing about competition is that there is a ceiling, a limit. When you hit it, you might cause more damage than any benefit the competition inspired. It makes you rethink the value of competition.

In our workshops and seminars, our goal is to help people, organizations and communities actualize their potential in positive ways. Competing with each other is the antithesis of what we do; we look for ways to coexist, to find solutions. At the same time, we are not against competition. Our goal is to promote healthy competition, the kind where you compete to the best of your ability in a spirit of respect. This was a core theme of The Pacific Institute® workshops with the U.S. Olympic Swim Team in 2008. Over a six week period, the coaches and swimmers trained and met with speakers such as Lou Tice and football coach Pete Carroll. They talked about competition and how it is meant to bring out the best in each other. A few weeks later, head coach Mark Schubert sent an email to Lou saying his two best swimmers, Michael Phelps and Ryan Lochte, had told him they never had so much fun in practice as they were having now. Is it coincidence that they went on to break record after record at the Summer Games in Beijing?

When coexistence is your goal, competition has a different tone. It is not about winning or coming in first; there is no race to finish because there is no end to the course of human existence. Competition becomes a place to excel, not destroy, because you are always respecting the human dignity of other competitors. It is a healthy balance between head and heart. It is an approach that lets you widen the gap between stimulus and response.

As crazy as it is, the Cold War MAD philosophy is a kind of coexistence. It has a number of fail safes built in to ensure there is a gap between stimulus and response. With such high stakes, you need that. We disagree with the notion that he who hesitates is lost. If coexistence is your goal, hesitation is the gap between stimulus and response; it is the difference between conflict and harmony. The hesitation gives you time to think of a better solution, time to remember there are two sides to every argument.

BUILDING YOUR EFFICACY

Bumps, barks and bings (conflict, anger and competition) are all part of the human experience, which makes them a part of the adventure of peaceful coexistence. You might be discomforted and challenged, but it is important not to let conflict, anger or competition frighten you. You do not want to bring fear along on your world peace adventure.

In order to deal effectively with the bumps, barks and bings you need to build your self-efficacy[27]. **Efficacy means to cause, bring about or make happen.** Martin Luther King had high efficacy: he was confident in his ability to cause or bring about change for African Americans. The Dalai Lama has high efficacy: he is confident in his ability to bring autonomy and peace to Tibet. Efficacy does not mean the desired goal will happen overnight or even in a lifetime. Dr. King was killed before the realization of his dream and the Dalai Lama has been working toward his goal for more than 40 years. Efficacious people are tough; they have the resilience and persistence necessary to push toward their goal, one step at a time.

> "Perceived self-efficacy is concerned not with the number of skills that you have, but with what you believe you can do with what you have under a variety of circumstances."
> - Dr. Albert Bandura, Self-efficacy: The exercise of control (1997)

WALLOW IN YOUR SUCCESS

Dr. Bandura[28] believes that most of us pass too quickly and too lightly through our successes. We do not spend enough time savoring, reviewing and recounting them. This prevents us from properly assimilated our successes, which in turn lessens the impact they could and should have in our lives. In your journey toward world peace, stop and celebrate every success. When Ron steps outside his comfort zone to help mediate an escalating conflict between two strangers, or when Gregg puts his chair between two verbal combatants in a planning session, it is peace in the making. It may be a small peace, but every peace counts. And every time you manage to put peace into action, you build your efficacy.

WELCOME TO GLOBAL CITIZENSHIP, MAKE US BETTER

One of the great things about seeing the adventure in coexistence is that it becomes easier to accept the ebb and flow of peace. Conflict is unavoidable, frustration and anger are inevitable, and competition will test the best of our ideals. But we need conflict to make progress. When ideas rub against each other, it creates a conflict in our mind. When faced with conflict, our minds naturally work toward a resolution. We resolve the conflict by running forward to deal with it; we leave it unresolved by running away from it. We make progress through the fire of resistance. Peace does not do away with that, but it does make the fire safe so we do not all get burned in an end-of-the-world inferno. It lets us work through conflict, anger and competition in a constructive way. It may feel like an uncomfortable, even unfriendly process, but that is the adventure. Throw yourself out of order to create the ideas and energy you need to reach your goals.

> *Gregg: As a Canadian, I was filled with pride to see our country host the 2010 Winter Olympics. I was drawn to the highs and lows, and to the pure emotion the Olympics creates. I particularly remember something John Furlong, the CEO of the Vancouver Olympic Organizing Committee, said at the opening ceremonies. He immigrated to Canada from Ireland as a young man. When he went through Customs, the officer behind the desk said, "Welcome to Canada, make us better." The phrase sticks with me, as do the images created by the Olympics. I remember a young Sikh with a turban on his head and a Canadian flag in his arms cheering and celebrating with friends. I remember the pictures of people of so many ethnicities gathered at the various venues, cheering and celebrating. That*

is the spirit I saw reflected at the 2010 Winter Olympics – millions of people from different cultures and backgrounds coming together to cheer for their home team, celebrating success and showing grace in defeat. Wow, welcome to global citizenship ... make us better.

DON'T JUST DO SOMETHING, STAND THERE

The human mind is designed to resolve issues – that's Gestalt. Despite the predictions of the end of the world, people keep finding ways to get along. That is the strange beauty of human evolution. We need disharmony and disorder to generate the energy to resolve the many challenges facing us. It is these challenge that build our efficacy and helps us move forward.

World peace is a big adventure. But a word of caution as you get ready to pick up the banner of peace. It is a great thing to march for peace, but you will need to balance "doing" things for peace with simply "being" in peace. Too often, we do things in the name of peace that are counter to peace. A march for peace turns into a clash between demonstrators and police, between "us" and "them". We want peace our way. So what is the right thing to do? Sometimes, you just don't know, because sometimes, there is no right thing to do. It is like trying to find the right words to say to someone whose spouse has been struck down by cancer, whose child has been killed in a drunk driving accident, whose home has been wiped out by a flood. People in these situations often say there are no right words, but that it does help if you can simply "be there" for them. There is wisdom in just being.

Peace as your goal will help you to become more mindful, and you will express that in your being. You will be more aware of times when you can "do" something and times when you just need to "be". Silence, calm, balance, being – that can be an adventure too.

REFLECTIVE QUESTIONS

- What constitutes adventure in your life?
- Do you have a worthy cause? If so, how do you describe the energy inside yourself about the cause?
- When have you been a peace-maker and why? Where did you miss an opportunity to make peace and why?
- How do you feel about conflict?
- What are the ways you can look at conflict positively?
- How do you defend your opinions? Does anger come up?
- Do people ever call you inflexible? Who, where, why?
- Can you create a space between stimulus and response?
- Do you set goals without knowing the how? Do you believe you can figure out? Do you believe it is a creative adventure?

"No pessimist ever discovered the secret of the stars, or sailed an uncharted land, or opened a new doorway to the human spirit.
Helen Keller – author, lecturer, political activist, deaf-blind person

PRINCIPLE 7:
OPTIMISM IS OUR CHOICE

You have the tools to look beyond your blindness, to challenge your normals and embrace coexistence. You are filled with love and ready for adventure. You are beginning to create a better world from the inside out. Now, how to sustain your transformation? We'll show you how to make optimism your choice.

World peace is optimistic, we know that. But we believe in striving for ideals. We might fail – a lot – but we keep trying because we are hopeful. We also believe optimism is our choice. This is the seventh and final principle of *World Peace, Really!*

> *Gregg: I admire Nelson Mandela. For me, he models many of the principles we talk about here, but especially love and especially optimism. How did he survive 27 years in prison in degrading and seemingly hopeless conditions? I think optimism played a role; it had to. The movie* Invictus *showed his optimism in action. As president of South Africa, Mandela*

used the national Springbok rugby team to create a common cause, something everyone – black and white – could cheer for. It wasn't easy because most black South Africans hated the team; it was seen as a symbol of apartheid. Somehow, his strategy succeeded. No, it wasn't a solution to all the scars of apartheid and it didn't resolve the divide between black and white, but it was a step toward forgiveness and reconciliation. At that time and in that place, that was optimistic. One of Mandela's inspirations is this poem, Invictus ("unconquerable"), which he kept in his cell.

> *Out of the night that covers me,*
> *Black as the pit from pole to pole,*
> *I thank whatever gods may be*
> *For my unconquerable soul.*
>
> *In the fell clutch of circumstance*
> *I have not winced nor cried aloud.*
> *Under the bludgeonings of chance*
> *My head is bloody, but unbowed.*
>
> *Beyond this place of wrath and tears*
> *Looms but the Horror of the shade,*
> *And yet the menace of the years*
> *Finds and shall find me unafraid.*
>
> *It matters not how strait the gate,*
> *How charged with punishments the scroll,*
> *I am the master of my fate:*
> *I am the captain of my soul.*

- William Ernest Henley (1849-1903)

CYNICS, IDEALISTS AND OPTIMISM

These days, it is a whole lot easier to be a cynic or naysayer than to be an optimist. The cynic finds reasons why peace is impossible. A lot of very intelligent people are content to be cynics. They are experts on what's wrong with the world. They use intelligent arguments and inescapable logic to outline pitfalls, problems and "why nots" – and then they leave you knee-deep in a swamp of negativity. Now you are in danger of falling into a downward spiral.

A downward spiral is a pattern of belief that prevents you from seeing the glass half full or hearing the good news. You reach a fail point in your life and feel paralyzed by your own lack of will. A study on the anatomy of depression shows three distinct thought patterns. It goes like this: I'm worthless, the world is hostile, I'm helpless. These thought patterns go round and round until your mind actually starts closing down avenues of thought. Hopeless, helpless, hostile. These negative feelings have direct access to your brain; continue down the path and you will begin to train your brain to only hear validation of the negative. This is the kind of depression you put yourself into. While not the same as clinical depression, it is just as real and just as dangerous.

DOWNWARD SPIRAL[29]

You expect to fail
You think people expect too much of you.
You have paralysis of will.
Your negative imagination runs wild.
You are isolated.

It is not just individuals who get into downward spirals – it is whole families, communities, companies and countries. Being caught in a downward spiral pattern is a formidable barrier to peace, and it happens within your own mind. When you feel depressed, you devalue yourself and those around you. Spouses devalue partners, parents devalue children, bosses devalue employees, one culture devalues another. You label, you dehumanize, you fail to respect the dignity and humanity of others. These are Bumps!, Bings! and Barks! – your own mental GPS letting you know that if you continue down this path you will not successfully reach your destination, be it peace in the world or peace at home.

Idealism is not synonymous with optimism, but it plays an important role. An optimist can be an idealist and a pragmatist at the same time. To be an idealist and an optimist can be affirming – just pay attention to what you are affirming. Not all ideals lead toward peaceful coexistence. Your ideal world might be one in which cultural diversity is widely accepted, or it might be one in which everyone believes in the same god, the same social etiquette, the same principles of government and so on. Take an honest look at the ideals you hold to be true, then ask yourself two questions. Do you believe they are positive ideals that can lead you to peaceful coexistence? Are they your North Star, do you navigate through life using these ideals … or are your eyes on your feet?

> *Gregg: When I first met Lou Tice in 1996, he asked me a question I will never forget. He said, "Are you an idealist?" I paused. My gut response was yes, but I wasn't sure that was the right answer. I didn't want to seem too naïve. After a few moments, I went with my gut and said, "Yes, I am." Looking back, I don't think there was a right or wrong answer for Lou; he just wanted to know if I was a good fit for The Pacific Institute. Lou believes in positive change. He believes human beings can reach their full potential and that communities can live in harmony. He's a pretty high-end idealist, but he's also a practical optimist.*

Optimism does not mean ignoring the harsh realities or the inherent complexities of the issues that trouble us. But where cynicism will lead you to a standstill, since there is no hope of resolving the issue, **optimism** will look for solutions. It will engage your mind, open your reticular activating system to see how issues might be resolved. It allows you to recognize partially right in other opinions, even when those opinions frighten you. It allows you to move forward rather than remain stuck. It allows you to listen to the cynics and say, "Okay, where are they partially right and how do we address that?" That's what Principle 7 is about: learning how to navigate through life by choosing optimism.

OPTIMISM IS A CHOICE BECAUSE OPTIMISM IS LEARNED

What does optimism as a choice look like? Look at Nelson Mandela, the Dalai Lama or Martin Luther King Jr. How about President John F. Kennedy's 1961 speech in which he committed the U.S.A. to landing a man on the moon and bringing him back safely before the end of the decade? It was certainly not the vision of a pessimist. The interesting point is that it was born out of the fear that Russia was winning the space race, a possibility military leaders saw as a direct threat to U.S. security. Yet Kennedy's vision was not military, it was scientific. Is it coincidence that after all these years, the U.S., Russians and other countries are working together on the International Space Station?

We believe optimism is a choice because we believe optimism is learned. This is the field in which Dr. Martin Seligman[30] has made such a notable impact. His theories on "learned helplessness" and "learned optimism" form the foundation of positive psychology, which is the study of optimal human functioning.

Ron: Martin Seligman once told me that he had a tendency to be a pessimist. I was so taken aback; I mean, this man is considered one of the giants of positive psychology! Yet he told me that by nature and by disposition he tends to be negative at first. On top of that, he says that as a scientist he is trained to look at things pessimistically. First you come up with a hypothesis, then you find ways to disprove it. To him, pessimism is an occupational hazard. He started by studying helplessness but ended up teaching us about optimism. Good for him.

YEAH, BUT...

Positive psychology has its detractors. For example, author Barbara Ehrenreich[31] believes our society has over-optimized to the point that we cannot deal with reality. Is she right? Well, according to integral theory she is partially right. We can coexist with that. Optimism is being willing to put forward an idea or ideal that you passionately believe in, and then accept that it might only be partially right. We passionately believe world peace is possible. But what if we are only partially right? Well, the compromise is coexistence. If we can coexist, we can start discussing the bigger issues in a more meaningful way.

Optimism does not mean building scotomas to issues of violence, hate, oppression, poverty, hunger and so on. Blinding yourself to the harsh realities of the world is just as monological as blinding yourself to the peaceful realities. The child mortality rate in some African countries, for example, remains unacceptably high and access to economic development unacceptably low. But child mortality and economic development rates are improving in most African countries. The "single story" of poverty is not an accurate one. As the Gapminder presentations show, the gap between rich and poor, developed and undeveloped is converging. It is a surprising lesson in optimism. If you remain skeptical about the possibility of world peace or even peaceful coexistence, consider this: you move toward what you think about. That is how your mind works. If you think peace is a hopeless cause, your reticular activating system will find all kinds of evidence to support the rightness of that viewpoint. If you think peace is possible, your RAS will find evidence to support that viewpoint.

Remember, you move toward what you think about; that is how your mind works.

HOW DO I CHOOSE OPTIMISM?

Dr. Seligman's research has found that human beings learn helplessness when they are unable to avoid negative experiences. One experience can lead to a broad perception of helplessness and lack of control, even when the power to control a situation is within a person's grasp. How many times have you listened to friends complain about a job they hate while privately wondering why they don't quit and move on to something new. They have the power to make that decision, but they have also learned to be helpless in the face of the repercussions, such as giving up the wage, benefits or pension. The core idea is that optimism can be learned. Whether you are a natural-born optimist or a natural-born pessimist, you can still choose optimism. We outline several steps to help you do that.

STEP #1: SET THE GOAL

If we want peace, we must make peace our goal – as a society but also as individuals. When you have a goal, your mind will start to move toward it and your reticular activating system will start to see it. If you see world peace, you see examples and opportunities for peace around you. You see peace. Without the goal, your scotomas remain. You can't see world peace, so you can't get world peace.

> *Gregg: I am sitting with about 10,000 other like-minded people listening to the Dalai Lama. Someone in the audience asks him how he would bring about world peace. His answer? Every time world leaders gather for a summit, he would have them come a week early. He would ask them to bring their spouses and children. Everyone would be a guest at the same resort or hotel. There would be no agenda. World leaders and their families would spend the week living and eating together. That was his plan. He chuckled, the way he does, and 10,000 people chuckled back. Of course, we thought! Let's get to know each other as moms and dads, husbands and wives, friends and neighbors – then let's talk.*

Remember, the goal comes first – your mind will move toward what you think about. Optimism is your choice, your goal. Use I x V = R: imagination x vividness = reality. Imagine yourself as an optimistic person; add emotion to make the image of your optimism vivid and clear. Replay this image in your mind, over and over, to make it real at the subconscious level. This simple exercise will help you challenge the habits, attitudes, beliefs and expectations that are hindering optimism.

SELF-REGULATION[32]

Self-regulation is adhering to an internal standard. It is neither good nor bad, or perhaps it is more accurate to say it can be both good and bad. If your internal standards push you to achieve bigger and bolder goals, and you self-regulate to that standard, good on you. Most people, however, do not self-regulate up, they self-regulate down, down to somewhere more comfortable, where that itchy dissonance feeling goes away. World peace demands that you self-regulate to your potential.

STEP #2: MANAGE YOUR SELF-TALK

Embedding a goal requires frequent reinforcement. If world peace is your goal, you need to remind yourself of this again and again, because you will move toward what you think and believe. Self-talk is a tool to get you there. Choose optimism by managing your self-talk. Self-talk is an act in which you evaluate or assess your behavior. It is how you talk to yourself when reacting to your own or others' evaluation of your performance, and it can have a profoundly positive or negative influence on your self-image. In Principle 4: Normal is Your Enemy we talked about "words-pictures-emotions" and how this pattern of thought is going on in your mind all the time. This is your self-talk. It creates your perception of normal. In order to change your perception, you have to challenge your self-talk.

> "If you pass on one important lesson to your children and grandchildren, teach them to manage their own self-talk."
> - Lou Tice, The Pacific Institute®

To control your self-talk you must become aware of it. Listen to the mutterings of your mind; a lot of it isn't very nice. As you become aware of your self-talk, you can choose to give sanction to it or to dispute it. Suppose you make a bad mistake at work. Is your self-talk saying, "I'm stupid" or is your self-talk saying, "That's not like me, next time I'll do better"? Do you sanction "I'm stupid" or dispute it with "That's not like me"? Controlling self-talk does not mean glossing over mistakes; as the U.S. Blue Angels say, if you make a mistake, "fess up and fix it".[33]

When it comes to peaceful coexistence, the test comes when you find yourself face to face with bad behavior. What is your self-talk saying? "I hate them." "People like that are bad." Who is in control here? You are. You do not have to excuse the behavior; the key is to not let your self-talk give sanction to negative labels and name-calling.

SELF-TALK YOURSELF INTO IT[34]

You literally accept how you describe yourself, which is why it is so important to eliminate negative self-talk. Eliminate the sarcasm, teasing, devaluation and belittling that go on in your mind. Instead of giving sanction to the negativity around you, become a disputer. Build positive goals and positive thoughts about your ability to achieve them.

STEP #3: USE AFFIRMATIONS TO CREATE AN UPWARD SPIRAL

As easily as your mind can fall into a negative way of thinking, you can talk yourself into an upward spiral. In an upward spiral, your brain is open and receptive to new ideas, new possibilities. So how do you keep your life in an upward spiral? You manage what you allow into your mind, you manage your self-talk to support a pattern of belief that life is welcoming, optimistic, valued. Affirmations are a tool we have seen work time and again. An affirmation is a statement of fact and/or belief. There are several components of an effective affirmation[35]:

- personal (use the word "I")
- action-oriented (defines "what")
- accurate (provides detail)
- present tense ("is" happening, not "will" happen)
- emotional (evokes a strong, positive emotion within you).

Write an affirmation about world peace using each of these components. If that seems too big, start with the principles. Build a positive affirmation about coexistence, overcoming blindness, embracing diversity, creating new normals, building your capacity for love, becoming more adventurous and choosing optimism. For example:

- I am a global citizen; it's exciting to practice coexistence every day.

- I recognize my opportunities to promote peace and it brings great joy and satisfaction to my life.

- I learn something new every day; I especially like busting my scotomas and the good energy that it releases.

- My life is full of new and interesting people; the more different you are, the more fascinating I find you.

- The world is changing for the better, because my world is changing for the better.

- I have a keen sense for how my humanity can make a positive difference in the world; I care about others even in moments of stress and conflict.

- I believe life is thrilling because I choose my adventures wisely; nothing is more satisfying than my own peace projects.

- I believe in the human race; happiness for me is seeing the good in other people – sometimes, regardless of their present circumstances.

Setting the goal, managing your self-talk and using affirmations can all help you choose optimism. You will find them effective tools for analyzing the steady stream of information coming at you, much of which is negative. The global media, in our point of view, is a big contributor to the downward spiral pattern of thinking. Media focus is on bad news: the latest crisis, natural disaster, random act of violence and so on. There are good news stories, but they are overwhelmed by the bad, which makes it seem like the bad news is winning. You need to exercise control over your mind and learn to dispute what you see, filter out the junk news, one-sided news and actively seek out the good news stories as well as the many different sides to various issues.

> *Ron: Several years ago, I attended a really cool event with Mayan elders and young leaders. One of the elders and I seemed to bond. He didn't speak English and I didn't speak Spanish or a Mayan dialect. It was all eye contact, smiles and body language. That tells me we don't need to speak the same tongue to speak peace. There's a saying, 'it's better to be quiet and thought stupid than to open your mouth and remove all doubt.' Maybe if we begin by just getting to know each other instead of jumping on our differences about religion and politics, we would have a better chance of coexistence. In fact, maybe if we just put our opinions in our back pocket, our humanity will shine through and carry us forward.*

Hard-line opinions and beliefs do not lend themselves well to optimism. The harder your opinions, the more entrenched you become in your normal and the easier it becomes to take a pessimistic view of conflict and change. In talking about world peace and coexistence, there are beliefs that neither of us is prepared to move on ... but that does not mean we cannot listen to or coexist with another point of view, nor does it mean we cannot be influenced.

BE PREPARED FOR A LITTLE "EUSTRESS"

Stress is a big factor in our ability to sustain optimism. Was Mahatma Gandhi stressed? How about the Dalai Lama, Martin Luther King Jr., Nelson Mandela? Given the magnitude of the changes they were calling for, you would think they would be overwhelmed by stress, and yet they were not. It reminds us of the famous Nietzsche quote, "He who has a strong enough why can bear any how."

One of the advances in cognitive science is the idea that there is both healthy stress and not-so-healthy stress. A researcher named Hans Selye[35] coined the term *eustress* to describe healthy stress. Eustress is good stress; it is the stress you feel as you move from one life stage to another. Reading this book may cause you to feel eustress. Taking on a new job, building a relationship with a new partner, travelling to different countries – all can cause eustress. Do not mistake this for something bad; this is good stress, it is a sign that you are evolving as a person.

> *Ron: I wake up in the middle of the night a lot, but very rarely is it from worry. More often than not, it is eustress. My creative juices are flowing – new goals, new projects. My creative subconscious is using dreamtime to solve problems. It's annoying, but I do recognize it as positive.*

Eustress is healthy stress. It gives you a feeling of fulfillment. It is a process of exploring potential gains.

SPIRAL DYNAMICS AND YOUR KOSMIC ADDRESS

Most of us do not consciously consider our identity as something meant to evolve, at least not once we are well into adulthood. If we did, we would not spend so much time and energy defending our Kosmic address of the moment (or some past moment) as the definitive "me" or "you". In reality, human identity is all about compromise and flexibility, about making the best of a bad situation or flourishing in a good situation. Our evolution is ongoing and optimistic. This is the basic premise of spiral dynamics[37], a theory developed and popularized in recent years by Don Beck, Ken Wilbur and others. Spiral dynamics has its advocates and its detractors; what we find interesting is the upward course it charts in human development.

WHERE DO YOU FIT?

Level one is simply about survival. At level two we come together to develop communities, cultures and beliefs. At level three, we become more hierarchical, we flex our muscles, build our power and use our strength to get what we want. Level four is where we evolve societies with distinct rules. The main driver at this level is conformity: we want to fit in. At level five we are expressing ourselves through our achievements in a conventional world. We're entrepreneurs, inventors, go-getters; we get satisfaction from achieving and acquiring material wealth. Theorists believe that most people's center of gravity is somewhere between level four (conformity) and level five (achieving). But some of us have attained level six, which is a more world-centric mindset. We begin to see humanity as part of one big family. We strive to achieve global goals like world peace and the elimination of hunger.

Just when we thought we had reached the peak, there is a whole other tier, a balcony that requires a significant leap. It has two levels. At the first level, we feel compelled to fulfill our lives, but we do not do so at the expense of other life. At the second level, we sacrifice our own self-interest in favor of a system that, apparently, is still evolving. This is the balcony to aspire to.

Spiral dynamics is one philosophy out of many that try to explain the human journey. We find it compelling, but we are not suggesting it is right or wrong; we simply use it to illustrate that the human race is in a state of growth. Your Kosmic address is changing every day; you are never in exactly the same place two days in a row, and that's okay. You are not supposed to be. Life is constantly unfolding around you. You can decide that you know all you need to know and close your mind; some people do make that choice. But it is contrary to who and what you are: the human mind is designed to grow, learn and evolve.

> *Ron: My friend John is an integral scholar who is always quick to remind me that growth and personal development is a choice. At his church, for example, he says there are people who picture God as a wise old man with a long white beard sitting on a cloud. These are good people. It is a reminder for me to get off my high horse and recognize that there is nothing right or wrong about where people are on their journey. The world may be evolving, but there are many places to live in God's universe.*

MAKING THE PARADIGM SHIFT

We believe human society is in the throes of a massive transformation. There is a spirit in the world that is evolving toward a higher level, call it God, call it the universe or what you will, but it has an energy and spirit of its own. It can be a time of great optimism or great pessimism. The common theme is that we are on the move toward something ... better, different, more complex?

Human evolution has never followed a linear path. There are paradigm shifts – a change in our fundamental belief that allows us to see the same information in a completely new way. History is full of paradigm shifts. In the last century, the Europeans felt the end of the world as they knew it was upon them ... because the world was running out of whale oil. Then came the paradigm shift to oil. Now our generation is looking at dwindling supplies of oil and guess what? There are those who foresee the end of the world as we know it, and those who see cause for optimism in our increasing development of bio-fuels and wind, solar and geothermal power. The fact is, every generation has left challenges for the generation that follows, and every generation has risen to the challenge beautifully. Somehow, the human race continues to find a way to adapt. Our children will fix what we screw up ... provided we let them. Call us optimistic.

We have no answers to the big questions. What we do have, and what we can share, is a simple, scientific way to make our world a better place. We can do it by managing our minds, choosing how we think and what we think about. We can do it by exercising control over how we talk to ourselves and to others, and by setting goals that expand our belief. Human beings are designed to solve problems – that's the adventure. How you, as an individual, determine to view the challenges will determine your behavior. If you chose optimism, you will move toward the challenge – we move toward what we think about. Let's think about world peace, really.

The point of our book is to demonstrate that change is possible, and that it begins in your own mind. We need to change how we think about world peace. We need to believe it is possible; we need to make it a personal goal; we need to affirm the goal and self-talk ourselves into it.

> *Ron: I occasionally use Facebook to throw curve balls to my friends. I might pose a provocative question, like "Who do you like to demonize?" One answer I got was, "Any Islamic fundamentalist". It made me wonder, what would happen if you're stuck alone in an elevator with an Islamic fundamentalist and neither of you can understand the other's language. Can you coexist? That is the question at the heart of it all: can we coexist with someone with whom we have a fundamental divide?*

WELCOME TO THE BALCONY

> *Gregg: I still remember the rush I got when I learned about spiral dynamics. I saw myself on level six. I was pretty proud about that. I thought, "Cool, I'm there!" Then I learned there were two more levels and thought, "Dang, I'm not there." But that's okay too, because there is a kind of exhilaration in knowing that there's more game to play.*

We began our dialogue about world peace by suggesting you imagine yourself on a balcony looking down at a dance floor – the dance floor of your life. The principles we have outlined here have helped you climb up onto the balcony. Now that you are here, what do you think of the view?

Welcome to the most exciting adventure on earth. World peace… really.

REFLECTIVE QUESTIONS

- Do you ever notice how well the world works? Just what do you see?
- Do you see the evolution in your life?
- What encourages you to be optimistic?
- What do you value now that you did not value 10 years ago?
- Where do you want to be 10 years from now?
- What are your visions for peace, really?
- What are your projects for peace, really?
- Who are your friends that care about peace, really?
- What is your next step, really?

"I have the audacity to believe that peoples everywhere can have three meals a day for their bodies, education and culture for their minds, and dignity, equality and freedom for their spirits."
Martin Luther King Jr., Nobel Peace Prize Acceptance Speech (1964)

REALLY.

World peace begins inside your mind and works its way out into the world. Your individual efficacy will add to our collective efficacy. Your individual commitment will add to our common cause. This is how world peace can happen ... by making a difference in own our backyards – our homes, schools, workplaces, communities, places of worship and so on.

Like Martin Luther King Jr., we have the audacity to believe that all of us on Planet Earth can have food for our bodies and learning for our minds and freedom for our spirits. We can peacefully coexist. We have combined our seven principles with the findings of cognitive psychology and The Pacific Institute's 40-year history of applying cognitive theory to the transformation of lives, communities and organizations.

Now it's your turn. You are nearing the end of the book, but we hope this is just the beginning of your journey. You have the knowledge and skills you need to advance the goal of world peace. Do something about it – at home, in your community, at work, online. We dare you … we double-dog dare you.

EFFICACY, CAUSE AND THE PEACE MATRIX

Before we send you out into the world, we want to underline the importance of efficacy and common cause in building world peace. We talked about building efficacy in Principle 6: Adventure is Our Friend. The bottom line of *World Peace, Really!* is that you need to believe world peace is possible. You need to believe in your own efficacy – your ability to cause, bring about or make happen. You also need a compelling "cause". We define a cause as a principle, desire or a movement that you are deeply committed to and that you are prepared to advocate and/or act for. World peace is the cause in our hearts, but there are many others. What is important to you? Ending hunger, eliminating racism, protecting the environment, ensuring affordable housing? If you look closely, you will realize that tackled together, different causes can add up to world peace.

A good cause needs to be clearly defined and have a compelling "why" attached to it. You must clearly understand why this is important, which means you need to be able to imagine it, give it vividness and make it real enough to embed in your subconscious. Remember – I x V = R. For example, when we began writing this book our cause of world peace almost overwhelmed us; it defied our ability to make it real. World peace is easy enough to say, but it is much harder to make vivid and real. So we took a step backward to peaceful coexistence. We could imagine peaceful coexistence in our own lives, in our communities, at our workplaces. And we could keep expanding it outward, from local to regional to national to global views. As we did, it become more vivid and real. That is the rich image we have embedded in our minds – peaceful coexistence.

Efficacy and cause are interrelated. For example, if you have a great cause with low efficacy (meaning you don't believe you can make a difference), how likely are you to really invest your time and energy into making it happen? How likely are you to leave it up to somebody else? Or, suppose you have high efficacy (meaning you know you can make things happen) but are not really sure about your cause. World peace may not be real to you – but how about peaceful coexistence in your community, can you contribute to that? We've illustrated the efficacy-cause relationship in the peace matrix. The ideal is the upper right quadrant: high efficacy, clear cause.

WHERE ARE YOU IN THE PEACE MATRIX?

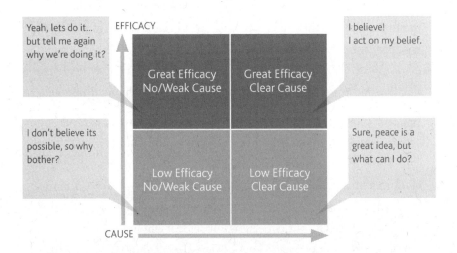

One of the interesting things about the peace matrix is that as you move closer to the ideal upper-right quadrant, your accountability grows. Instead of waiting for someone else to make peace, you begin to seize opportunities to make peace in your own life. Self efficacy

– the belief in your ability to make something happen – becomes a driver of peace in your own life as well as in your community.

Develop clarity on your cause. Clarity will help you define the "why" behind the "what". What you want is world peace, but why do you want it? Answering the "why" will strengthen your conviction, which in turn will help increase your efficacy. A strong "why" can also build a common cause and increase collective efficacy. But the goal comes first, always. Define your goal, make it clear, use affirmations and self-talk to increase your efficacy. Doing these things will help you get to the upper right-hand quadrant of the peace matrix.

> When we develop COLLECTIVE EFFICACY with a COMMON CAUSE, we exponentially elevate our ability to make our cause happen.

THE CHARACTERISTICS OF SUCCESS: POSITIVE DEVIANCE

In every sector of society, there are individuals who seem to perform at a higher level than others. People who seem to have a clear line of sight on what they believe they need to do – and who do it. These people are positive deviants[38] (emphasis on the last syllable, dai-vai-awnts) and they live on the far right of the standard bell curve. A positive deviant is someone who is able to forge ahead despite setbacks, who doesn't seem to take setbacks personally, who models both efficacy and cause. They are also the people you want to model yourself after. Jeremy Gilley is one example who leaps to mind. An actor and filmmaker by profession, he is the man who spearheaded the drive to have the United Nations declare a global ceasefire and non-violence day. He succeeded. In 2001, 192 member states unanimously adopted September 21st as the International Day of Peace. Gilley did not achieve this alone. He used his passion to build a common cause with collective efficacy to achieve the goal of one day of peace. Gilley is a positive deviant.

Worth a Visit:
Gilley's Peace One Day project is attempting to introduce 3 billion people to Peace Day by 2012. Learn more about what you can do to help at www.peaceoneday.org

(-) DEVIANT	NORMAL	(+) DEVIANT
LOW AVERAGE:	HIGH AVERAGE:	POSITIVE DEVIANT:
Apathetic	Engaged	**Purposeful**
Pessimistic	Optimistic	**Focused on Others**
Cynical	Participating	**Self-Driven/ Self-Reliant**
Monological	Pluralistic	**Courageous**
Low Efficacy	Higher Efficacy	**High Efficacy**

Positive deviants are purposeful, focused on others, self-driven/self-reliant, courageous and highly efficacious. These traits are ingredients for success in any endeavor, including world peace. And they are traits we can all nurture within ourselves.

A DOUBLE-DOG DARE

You have the cause, the conviction and the efficacy. Now add action to the picture. Consider it our double-dog dare. Take what you have learned in the seven principles to become a positive deviant in the cause of peace. Support a peace project big or small, or start one of your own.

Do you think you can make a difference? This question is where many of us stumble, but sometimes making a difference is simply about offering a fresh point of view, one based on peaceful coexistence. A recent example: Ron received an email from a friend that contained a collection of inflammatory quotes by a number of high profile people regarding ethnicity and race in America. The email was being widely disseminated. Our intent is not to make you curious about the quotes themselves. They are actually irrelevant to the point we are making and we are not going to repeat them here. We have also taken the specific ethnic identity out of the argument. In place of the quotes, we want you to imagine an intolerant viewpoint you've heard passed around at the office, read in media editorials or seen in online forums. With what you have heard, read or seen echoing in your mind, consider the email dialogue between Ron and his friend.

Friend's comment to Ron on the mass email containing inflammatory quotes:

> RON – THIS IS ONE OF MANY REASONS I HAVE FEARS FOR OUR COUNTRY – THE WORLD IS NOT WHAT WE GREW UP IN.

Ron's comment to friend:

> DON...I PERSONALLY BELIEVE THIS EMAIL IS DANGEROUS...IT DOES NOT REPRESENT A REASONED ARGUMENT, IT IS ONE-SIDED... IT IS MEAN AND IN SOME PLACES IT COULD BE CONSIDERED RACIST...THIS IS NOT GOOD CITIZENSHIP, IN MY OPINION...THERE ARE BETTER WAYS TO TACKLE THE IMPORTANT SUBJECT OF IMMIGRATION POLICY.

Friend's response

> I RESPECT YOUR VIEWS – HOW DO YOU DEAL WITH A PERSON OR PERSONS THAT DO NOT POSSESS YOUR VALUES OR VIEWS BUT ENJOYS THE BENEFITS OFFERED TO HIM IN THIS GREAT COUNTRY – I WATCHED COACH _____ STATE THAT THERE WERE 5 PLAYERS NOT ON THE TEAM BECAUSE THEY DID NOT BUY INTO THE PROGRAM – HE COULD NOT HAVE THEM ON THE TEAM BECAUSE THEY ARE A CANCER – I BELIEVE THIS IS TRUE IN OUR COUNTRY YOU ARE – OR – YOU ARE NOT ON THE TEAM – I DON'T SEE A WINNING COMBINATION HERE FROM THE [ETHNIC] LEADERSHIP.

Ron:

> THE QUOTES ON THE EMAIL ARE A LIMITED SELECTION...DON'T YOU THINK SOMEONE COULD PUT TOGETHER A LIST OF ADMIRABLE

QUOTES FROM ADMIRABLE [ETHNIC] LEADERS JUST AS EASILY? MAYBE NOT. BEING A CITIZEN, AND BEING A CITIZEN OF COLOR, IS NOT LIKE BEING ON A FOOTBALL TEAM...IT'S MORE COMPLEX. HOW DO WE DEAL WITH IT ALL? GOAL SET TO LISTEN, TO COEXIST, REALIZE ON COMPLEX ISSUES THAT THERE IS MORE THAN ONE TRUTH (PERSPECTIVE). MY OPINION. WHAT I REALLY OBJECT TO PERSONALLY IS THE ANGRY, FEARFUL, NASTY, LASH-OUTS — BY EITHER SIDE ...THAT COULD BE ANOTHER FORM OF CANCER, MORE LETHAL.

Friend:

I AGREE

It is easy to let this kind of email slide. But when you are clear on what really matters to you, you find the courage to respond. These are the small opportunities for making peace – or making a difference to peaceful coexistence – that come our way every day. So often, peace begins not with the big grand gestures but with a series of smaller, often uncomfortable, often awkward attempts to provide another point of view in the face of someone else's anger and fear. This is why it is so important to clarify what you believe in and why. Building clarity on peaceful coexistence will open your reticular activating system to opportunities to model it – and every one of these attempts to model what you believe translates into you making a difference.

APPLY THE SEVEN PRINCIPLES

What happens when you receive an email or see a news story that seeks to spread intolerance and fear? For many of us, the response is often a sinking, sick feeling. Instead of letting it pass, try applying the seven principles.

1. Coexistence is our goal: where do inflammatory and prejudice communications lead, towards the goal or away from the goal?

2. Blindness is our problem: is what you are hearing a single story? Is there a partially right here? What other partially rights have been left out? Do the people behind the story have scotomas?

3. Diversity is our strength: does this story promote diversity or seek to create conformity? Are you disputing the information coming in or silently accepting it?

4. Normal is our enemy: what is being normalized in this story? What threshold is being crossed, what new normal is being created?

5. Love is our journey: is this non-judgment and forgiveness or is the judgment and grudgment?

6. Adventure is our friend: is this a Bump!, Bark! or Bing!? When you read this, does it trigger fear/threat or does it suggest options/possibilities?

7. Optimism is our choice: is this story optimistic? Does it hold out hope that we are moving toward a more peaceful world? Can you climb the balcony to attain a broader viewpoint?

IT'S TIME TO START YOUR JOURNEY

Clarify what matters to you. If you find world peace too big a concept, focus on issues that really matter to you. Ask yourself why it matters; why do you care? Explore your reasons and build your conviction. Now start looking for opportunities for more peaceful coexistence? You might find inspiration in one of the United Nations eight Millennium Goals[39], such as eradicating extreme poverty and hunger. Maybe you cannot end world hunger, but you can drop a donation off at your local food bank and help end hunger in your community. Progress on any one of these issues will help move our world towards peaceful coexistence.

Build your efficacy. Build your efficacy in the cause of peace, and you will become part of the common cause, the common spirit that is moving us toward greater peace. It will not happen overnight, but it will happen in ways that will surprise you. The day the Berlin Wall came down was a day like any other – until the wall came down. People were hoping it would come down, they even expected it to come down, but not on that particular day. And that made the mood all the more jubilant. Peace had won. Every day around the world, peace erupts in unexpected places and in unexpected ways. There is still conflict and violence in the world, there is still legitimate anger over things done and not done. Anger is part of our human face; it is our reaction to things that frighten us, that seem out of our control. But now that you have a better understanding of how to manage your mind, you can also make conscious choices about anger. You no longer need to swallow it or be swallowed by it. Use the skills you have learned to deal with it constructively. Grow your efficacy.

Throw yourself out of order. It doesn't have to be anything life altering – but then again, it can be. The point is to do something different that puts you outside your comfort zone.

WHAT NEXT?

We are going to leave you with a practice we learned from Lou and Diane Tice. After a day of seminars, Lou would get everyone together over dinner. As a way to break the ice and get people talking, he would ask everyone to name a new person they had met who had had the most influence on them over the last year and why. It was always moving to hear people's answers.

Imagine yourself at a similar dinner, except the main topic of conversation is peace. When your turn comes, who will you say has had the most influence on your belief in peace over the past year and why? Who helped throw you out of order, shake up your beliefs, open your RAS, uncover your blind spots? But wait, we're not quite finished. Imagine yourself at another dinner a year from now. The question is asked and you are listening to the responses.

How would you feel if someone stood up and named … you?

EPILOGUE

THE PACIFIC INSTITUTE

We have been privileged to be part of The Pacific Institute® (TPI) team, Ron for over 30 years, Gregg for over 15. We have drawn freely on many TPI concepts in this book – and we want to give credit where credit is due. TPI has been taking the findings of cognitive psychology and translating them into practical applications for 40 years. We have the track record to prove that it works. You do not need to take our word for it, visit the TPI website and see for yourself.

We also want to emphasize that the TPI concepts introduced in this book are just that – introductions. We have been living and breathing TPI concepts for so long, it comes naturally to us, but there's so much richness here. We touch on the basics – there's a lot more depth behind each of these concepts. TPI also has contributing information on implementation strategies and specific case studies that help make up the whole.

Check out TPI Global News for videos and stories on some of the exciting TPI projects happening around the world. **www.thepacificinstitute.com**

WANTED: 1,000 PEACE PROJECTS

Are you looking for a more active way to get involved in world peace? Good, because we are looking for 1,000 peace projects. Visit www.worldpeacereally.com for more information.

What is a peace project? Here's our definition: a peace project is an attempt by a group, organization or community to anticipate or deal with discord, disharmony, discontent or outright conflict in a constructive way. It might be discord in your workplace, tension in your school, conflict in your community. It might be a family feud or a neighborhood quarrel. We would like to hear how the principles in *World Peace, Really* helped on your journey toward peaceful coexistence.

If you're living in an unresolved situation and are looking for help, call us. If you're an organization in the peacemaking community, a community group seeking to build collective efficacy, or a socially responsible business or businessperson looking to play a bigger role in creating a better world, invite us in. We will facilitate the learning process and start you on your own journey to world peace … really.

Be one of our 1,000 peace projects.
We double-dog dare you – it will be an adventure!
1-800-426-3660

ENDNOTES

1. Lou Tice, *Smart Talk for Achieving Your Potential: 5 Steps to Get You from Here to There* (The Pacific Institute, 2007)
2. Lou Tice, *Smart Talk*
3. ibid.
4. ibid.
5. Erik Erikson, *Identity and the Life Cycle* (W.W. Norton & Company, 1994)
6. Chimamanda Ngozi Adichie, *The Danger of the Single Story*, http://www.ted.com/speakers/chimamanda_ngozi_adichie.html (October 2009)
7. Lou Tice, *Smart Talk*
8. Ken Wilbur, *Integral Psychology: Consciousness, Spirit, Psychology, Therapy* (Shambhala; 1st paperback edition, May 16, 2000)
9. Ken Wilber, "The Ways We Are in This Together: Intersubjectivity and Interobjectivity in the Holonic Kosmos" Excerpt C of draft of forthcoming book, *Kosmic Karma and Creativity*, http://wilber.shambhala.com/html/books/kosmos/excerptC/intro-1.cfm/
10. Lou Tice, *Smart Talk*
11. Chris Rock, interviewed on CBC *Q with Jian Ghomeshi*, October 15, 2009, http://www.cbc.ca/q/episodes/
12. Ted Falcon, Don Mackenzie and Jamal Rahman, *Getting to the Heart of Interfaith: The Eye-opening, Hope-filled Friendship of a Pastor, a Rabbi and a Sheikh*, Skylight Paths Publishing, June 2009)
13. Rosling's presentations can be seen on www.TED.com or www.gapminder.org
14. Lou Tice, *Smart Talk*
15. Get the full text of President Obama's speech at www.whitehouse.gov (click on Speeches & Remarks under Briefing room, then select Remarks by the President at the University of Michigan Spring Commencement, May 1, 2010.

16 Glenna Gerard and Linda Ellinor, "Dialogue: Something Old, Something New", www.thedialoguegrouponline.com

17 Lou Tice, *Smart Talk*

18 J.F. Rischard, *High Noon: 20 Global Problems, 20 Years to Solve Them* (Basic Books, May 2003)

19 Human Security Brief 2006, http://www.humansecuritybrief.info/2006/media.html

20 Stephen Covey, *The 8th Habit: From Effectiveness to Greatness* (Free Press, November 2004)

21 http://adr.navy.mil/content/principles.aspx

22 Lou Tice, *Smart Talk*

23 ibid.

24 ibid.

25 ibid.

26 ibid.

27 ibid.

28 Dr. Bandura's theories have been well published. His books include *Social Foundations of Thought and Action: A Social Cognitive Theory (1986)* and *Self-efficacy: The exercise of control (1997)*.

29 Lou Tice, *Smart Talk*

30 Dr. Seligman is the author of several books, including *Learned Optimism: How to Change Your Mind and Your Life*. Listen to Martin Seligman's talk on positive psychology at www.TED.com

31 Barbara Ehrenreich, *Bright-sided: How the Relentless Promotion of Positive Thinking Has Undermined America* (Metropolitan Books, October 2009)

32 Lou Tice, *Smart Talk*

33 ibid.

34 ibid.

35 ibid.

36 Hans Selye, *The Stress of Life* (McGraw Hill, 2nd edition, March 1978)

37 Don Edward Beck and Christopher C. Cowan, *Spiral Dynamics: Mastering Values, Leadership and Change* (Wiley-Blackwell, paperback edition, July 2005); Wilbur, *Integral Psychology*

38 There is an entire website devoted to Positive Deviance at www.positivedeviance.org

39 Check out all 8 of the United Nations Millennium Development Goals at http://www.un.org/millennium/declaration/ares552e.htm

INDEX

7-Eleven 20, 44, 105

A

Adichie, Chimamanda Ngozi 151
affirmations 44, 130, 141
ah-ha 9, 15, 16, 69, 160
ANNIKA Golf Academy 67
apartheid 121
attitudes 6, 9, 21, 22, 51, 68, 69, 88, 127
Avery 111, 161

B

balcony 12, 13, 75, 78, 133, 136, 146
Bandura, Al 11
barbershop 96, 105
Bark! 111, 146
bear story 80
Beck, Don 133
beliefs 6, 9, 10, 16, 17, 18, 19, 21, 23, 28, 30, 32, 34, 35, 37, 39, 48, 50, 56, 57, 59, 68, 70, 72, 73, 74, 76, 82, 88, 98, 104, 109, 127, 131, 133, 148, 161
Bing! 75, 79, 112, 146
Brogen 111, 161
Bump! 109, 146
Bush, George W. 56

C

Calli 94, 160
Carroll, Pete 114
citizenship 26, 58, 117
Clinton, Bill 74
Coexist Index 51, 52
cognitive dissonance 106
cognitive psychology 6, 8, 12, 17, 138, 149
Cold War 15, 16, 17, 20, 65, 92, 113, 114, 160
comfort zone 48, 52, 53, 67, 104, 106, 115, 147
common cause 121, 138, 139, 141, 147
conscious 19, 21, 22, 68, 69, 71, 87, 98, 147

Covey, Stephen 96, 152
creative subconscious 21, 22, 23, 35, 68, 69, 71, 100, 105, 132

D

Dalai Lama 24, 115, 124, 127, 131
Darwin, Charles 54
dehumanize 25, 41, 60, 95, 123
depression 122
détente 21, 23
dialogue 10, 48, 49, 59, 60, 107, 109, 136, 143
Discovering the Power in Me™ 110
discussion 10, 48, 59, 87
dispute 10, 48, 56, 57, 87, 104, 128, 131
dissonance 72, 73, 76, 81, 100, 105, 106, 127
double-dog dare 139, 143, 150
downward spiral 122, 130

E

efficacy 7, 11, 115, 116, 117, 138, 139, 140, 141, 143, 147, 150, 152
ego identity 24, 25, 37, 50
Ehrenreich, Barbara 152
Ellinor, Linda 59, 152
Erikson, Erik 24, 151
eustress 106, 132
expectations 9, 23, 68, 71, 88, 127

F

F card exercise 35, 36, 56
forgiveness 85, 86, 87, 95, 102, 121, 146

G

Gallup 51, 52
Gapminder 125
generativity 24
Gerard, Glenna 59, 152
gestalt 9, 71, 72, 93, 100, 117
Gilley, Jeremy 141
global citizenship 117
goal-oriented 99
goal setting 9, 111
Golden Rule 90

Gorbachev, Mikhail 14, 15, 20, 74
grudgment 85, 87, 146

H

habits 9, 22, 68, 69, 85, 88, 127
Henley, William Ernest 121
Human Security Report 92

I

Idealism 123
integral theory 36, 56, 125
interfaith amigos 49
International Day of Peace 142
Invictus 120, 121
I x V = R 99, 127, 139

K

Katelyn 111, 161
Kennedy, President John F. 124
King, Martin Luther Jr. 57, 87, 88, 124, 131, 138
Kosmic address 37, 78, 132, 133

L

Latham, Dr. Soosan 106
learned helplessness 57, 124
learned optimism 57, 124, 152
legitimate anger 89, 147
lock-on/lock-out 36, 56
Love Leadership 67, 161

M

MAD 20, 64, 65, 113, 114
Mandela, Nelson 57, 96, 120, 124, 131
Martin Luther King Jr. 57, 87, 88, 124, 131, 138
Millennium Goals 147, 153
monological 40, 41, 125
mutual assured destruction 65

N

National Football League 112
non-judgment 85, 87, 90, 146
Northern Ireland 5, 19, 72
nuclear weapons-free world 66

O

Obama, Barack 39, 48, 56, 61, 80
Olympics 33, 116, 117
out of order 73, 106, 116, 147, 148

P

partially right 27, 38, 39, 40, 42, 56, 60, 75, 104, 112, 124, 125, 146
peace matrix 140, 141
positive deviant 141, 142, 143
positive psychology 124, 125, 152, 160
Powell, Colin 14, 15, 16, 20
President John F. Kennedy 124
PX2 23

R

RAS 108, 109, 110, 126, 148
requisite variety 54
reticular activating system 107, 108, 109, 124, 126, 145
Rischard, J.F. 92, 152
Rock, Chris 151
Rosling, Hans 50

S

sanction 56, 57, 58, 128, 129
Sandra 19, 43, 111, 161
sanity 21, 22, 35, 66, 85, 100
Saudi Arabia 9, 42, 52
scotoma 35, 36, 41, 44, 45, 50
scotoma-busting 44, 45, 50
self-efficacy 115
self-talk 17, 25, 57, 111, 128, 129, 130, 135, 141
Seligman, Martin 57, 125, 152
Selye, Hans 152
September 21st 142
spiral dynamics 136
stimulus and response 96, 97, 114, 118
Stone, Oliver 56
subconscious 21, 22, 23, 35, 68, 69, 70, 71, 78, 80, 85, 99, 100, 105, 127, 132, 139
Summer Night Lights 23

T

TED 30, 31, 50, 93, 106, 151, 152
The Pacific Institute 5, 12, 23, 57, 123, 138, 149, 151, 159, 160, 161
threshold 76, 77, 78, 146
Tice, Diane 147
Tice, Lou 12, 114, 123, 128, 151, 152
TPI 8, 9, 12, 33, 57, 99, 149, 159, 160
truths 9, 18, 21, 22, 30, 35, 39, 42, 46, 60, 68, 104

U

United Nations 42, 48, 66, 89, 141, 147, 153
U.S. Blue Angels 128
U.S. National Swim Team 33
U.S. Navy 97

W

Wilbur, Ken 133, 151
Words-pictures-emotions 71, 99, 128

ACKNOWLEDGEMENTS

In writing *World Peace Really*, our first big thank must go to Beverley Fast, our co-writer. The smooth and flowing narrative linking the many concepts, principles and theories belongs to Bev. You make reading a joy.

A second thank you goes to all our "readers", our loving critics. You know who you are. We received valuable feedback and suggestions, many of which have been incorporated into the book. It only hurt a little bit and often made us laugh.

And, again, a thank you to The Pacific Institute, especially the hundreds of affiliates, partners, project directors and field consultants who have built the TPI body of work over the last 40 years. You are the unsung heroes and heroines, until now.

Most importantly, thank you to our families. Your love, support and patience made this project possible.

Thank you, all. The best is yet to come…really.

ABOUT THE AUTHORS

L to R: Ron Medved and Gregg Cochlan

Ron Medved is an athlete, artist and social entrepreneur businessman who grew up during the height of the Cold War era and still remembers hiding under his desk during nuclear attack drills in grade school.

"The Cold War had a huge influence on my childhood. It was frustrating being half-scared of what might or could happen and I remember wishing the world could be different." Coming of age in the turbulent 1960s opened Ron to looking at the world, and his role in it, in new ways. His own journey has taken him from All-American football player to stockbroker to project director to VP of business development and now a special projects affiliate with The Pacific Institute (TPI).

Through TPI and his own consulting practice, Ron has seen the impact of positive psychology on personal and organizational performance, and he believes it has equal potential to impact peaceful coexistence. "*World Peace, Really* is an audacious project, but Gregg and I have the experience to back it up. The book draws on established findings in human psychology to promote the cause of peace. The focus is very personal. The ah-ha moment comes when you realize that peace starts inside your own mind and heart."

Ron and his wife Calli make their home near Seattle, in his home state of Washington. He has two adult children: Shawn and Erin and two granddaughters, Breanne and Madison.

Gregg Cochlan is an author, consultant and leadership coach whose first book, Love Leadership, *challenged traditional corporate conditioning by positioning love as a more effective leadership style.*

"People think it's daring to say world peace really is possible, but it's actually a logical next step after telling corporate leaders that leading with love is better for your bottom line." Gregg traces his willingness to challenge traditional norms to his small town upbringing. He learned early that women can be sheriffs, that childhood friends are for life, that diversity is more fun than homogeny, that the more you give the more you get, that it's important to be comfortable being uncomfortable and, finally, that love triumphs over all.

A need to make a bigger difference led Gregg to The Pacific Institute, to Love Leadership and now to World Peace, Really. "I'm optimistic about the ability of human beings to solve problems, but I recognize that the world is getting smaller. That's creating more potential for conflict – more polarization of beliefs, politics and norms. The seven principals in our book are practical, applicable ways to get past conflict and achieve peaceful coexistence. It's cognitive science coming to the rescue."

Gregg and his wife Sandra live in the wide open spaces of Saskatoon, Saskatchewan, Canada. They have three children, Katelyn, Avery and Brogen.